W9-ABB-178

ENDORSEMENTS FOR
WOMEN FOR AFGHAN WOMEN

"The women speaking in this remarkable and timely book are as diverse a group as you could find anywhere: writers, activists, feminists, theologians, journalists, professors; women of different cultures, religions, ethnicities, languages, and, most important, women of widely varying opinions. If we listen to them with open minds, we will learn a lot about acceptance and about how to effect change for women in the world without arousing resentment."
— Radhika Coomaraswamy, United Nations Special
Rapporteur on Violence Against Women

"It is essential that the women of Afghanistan, after being systematically oppressed and disregarded by the Taliban, be at the core of decision making in the new government. The writing in this book gives testament to the brilliance, power and potential of the women of Afghanistan. These voices must be heard."
— Eve Ensler, author of *The Vagina Monologues* and *Necessary Targets*

"This excellent and timely collection of essays illuminates many issues of pressing importance. Over the last year many people have spoken on behalf of Afghan women; this book serves the invaluable function of allowing them to speak for themselves."
— Amitav Ghosh, author of *The Glass Palace*

"Throughout history and in many nations, women's power has been seriously limited by the circumstances of their daily lives. They need great strength and courage to overcome these obstacles and move beyond a position of helplessness. Many Afghan women have risen above the repression of the recent regimes to become a driving force in the reshaping of their country. This important volume dispels many of the myths surrounding the Afghan people and their history and shows us, once more, that women's participation is not only right and essential, but vital."
— Ambassador Swanee Hunt, Director of the Women and Public Policy Program,
John F. Kennedy School of Government, Harvard University

"Women have resisted oppression everywhere and throughout history. But some survival stories make history. In this regard the women in Afghanistan and refugee Afghan women worked in the shadows to preserve their dignity. They did not expect mercy or support. Their only goal was to escape the damage of humiliation. The experience must have left behind scars but it has given them wisdom and strength. They know, more than anyone else, the value of freedom. Women from all regions of the world are paying homage to this courageous species of human beings. I commend the members of Women for Afghan Women for this illuminating collection of essays."
— Asma Jahangir, Advocate Supreme Court of Pakistan, Human Rights
Commission of Pakistan, UN Special Rapporteur

"This book is a must read for anyone with questions regarding Muslim women. The emergence of Afghan women speaking for themselves with clarity, passion, and a vision for the future is heartening. Since September 11th, terms like *jihad, fundamentalism, burqa,* and others, are being increasingly used, often incorrectly. This book provides the proper framework for these terms, and once you start reading, you'll be so engaged that you'll finish it in one sitting. I recommend it highly."
— Dr. Faroque Khan, author of *Story of a Mosque in America*
and Spokesperson for the Islamic Center of Long Island

"Throw away clichéd ideas of Afghan women as passive, silent victims cowering under their burqas. The voices collected here—energetic, passionate, knowledgeable and wise—are the ones the world needs to hear if Afghanistan is to achieve real peace and solve its many problems."
—Katha Pollitt, Nation columnist and author of *Subject to Debate: Sense and Dissents on Women, Politics, and Culture*

"For many women around the world their first introduction to Afghanistan was the suffering (plight) of Afghan women under the Taliban regime. But once that message trickled out, American and American-Afghan women mounted such an effective campaign, that almost single handedly they played a major role in turning around the former Clinton administration's soft pedaling on the Taliban regime and they also influenced other Western governments to review their Afghan policy—well before September 11. Many of these brave women who were responsible for this extraordinary feat are represented in this book, as are new comers who awoke to the repression of the Taliban regime on September 11. Women were responsible for mobilizing international public opinion against the Taliban and for rescuing Afghanistan. This book ensures that their story is told, that their struggle is not forgotten and that it continues as Afghan women try and rebuild their shattered lives and country."
—Ahmed Rashid, author *of The Resurgence of Central Asia: Islam or Nationalism?* and *Taliban*

"For decades images of Afghan women have been manipulated as symbols by male dominated political groups. In this book Afghan women, mostly those who have been forced to seek refuge abroad, tell their own stories of these decades of violence and how they hope to transform their own societies. They are passionate about the need for education and dialogue as means for peaceful transformation, and in these writings they offer the reader just such an education and dialogue."
—Barnett Rubin, author of *The Fragmentation of Afghanistan* and *The Search for Peace in Afghanistan*

"If you read only one book this year on Afghanistan, let it be this one. For the first time, American readers who are concerned about the effects on women of the U.S. war against terrorism and who want to know more about the history, present condition, and plans and possibilities for the women of Afghanistan no longer need to rely on the words and agendas of American feminists alone. In *Women for Afghan Women,* we leave behind us the racist stereotype of passive victim beneath the burqa and hear instead the concise articulation of a nation of women standing on the edge of their own futures, ready to take on a new world. As Sima Wali notes in her foreword, '...there are solutions which can come only from within the Afghan community.' Without the voices in this book, the many and varied voices of Afghan women, there is no 'new Afghanistan.' These women and their men and children are the new Afghanistan."
—Sapphire, author of *Push* and *Black Wings & Blind Angels*

"This stimulating collection gives a voice to women whose voices have been shrouded in silence. To read the words of many of these remarkable women is to understand the truth behind—and beyond—the burqa."
—Shashi Tharoor, author of *Riot* and Head of the Department of Public Information, United Nations

WOMEN FOR AFGHAN WOMEN

Shattering Myths and Claiming the Future

EDITED BY

Sunita Mehta

WITH ASSISTANCE FROM

Esther Hyneman, Batya Swift Yasgur, and Andrea Labis

palgrave
macmillan

WOMEN FOR AFGHAN WOMEN
Copyright © Sunita B. Mehta, 2002. Individual chapters copyright ©
individual authors.
All rights reserved. No part of this book may be used or reproduced in
any manner whatsoever without written permission except in the case of
brief quotations embodied in critical articles or reviews.

First published 2002 by
PALGRAVE MACMILLAN™
175 Fifth Avenue, New York, N.Y. 10010 and
Houndmills, Basingstoke, Hampshire, England RG21 6XS.
Companies and representatives throughout the world.

PALGRAVE MACMILLAN is the global academic imprint of the
Palgrave Macmillan division of St. Martin's Press, LLC and of Palgrave
Macmillan Ltd. Macmillan® is a registered trademark in the United
States, United Kingdom and other countries. Palgrave is a registered
trademark in the European Union and other countries.

ISBN 1–4039–6052–6 hardback
ISBN 1–4039–6017–8 paperback

Library of Congress Cataloging-in-Publication Data
is available from the Library of Congress.

A catalogue record for this book is available from the British Library.

Design by Letra Libre, Inc.

First edition: Pub Month Year
10   9   8   7   6   5   4   3   2

Printed in the United States of America

This book is dedicated

in love to my family, whose unwavering support helps me believe that I am capable of the impossible:

Mum, Dad, Mummi, Pappa, Suketu,
Anand, Sejal, Monica, Gautama, Akash

in respect and camaraderie to Fahima Danishgar, cofounder of Women for Afghan Women, as well as all the members and supporters of Women for Afghan Women. Our joint commitment will see us through the long road ahead.

in gratitude to Helen, Kanyere, Ann, and Kaliah of The Sister Fund, whose generosity and faith in me led to the birthing of this organization.

in sisterhood, above all, to Afghan women in Afghanistan and throughout the world:

We hope this book inspires you to
speak, write, agitate, and dream.
The future is yours.

SPECIAL THANKS TO:

Gayatri Patnaik of Palgrave/St. Martin's Press—without whom there would be no book.

Patricia Clough, Elizabeth Small, and the Women's Studies Certificate Program at the Graduate Center of the City University of New York—for hosting the conference that led to this book.

The Sister Fund, the Global Fund for Women, the North Star Fund, the New York Women's Foundation, and the Hunt Alternatives Fund—for financial support.

SAKHI for South Asian Women—our sisters, and our fiscal sponsors.

Purvi Shah—for helping to conceptualize this book, and to Marti Copleman for supporting its production in very many ways.

Robina Niaz, Homaira Mamoor, and Zarina Mustapha—for help with editing the pieces on Islam.

Asra Malikzay—for help in the search for Afghan women poets.

Mustafa Siddiq—for bringing ideas, friends, and resources to the rescue each time a problem threatened to present itself.

And every individual and organization that has supported our work—there are too many to name.

CONTENTS

Section Two
Stories and Strategies for Claiming the Future

EDITOR'S PREFACE

THE DEBUT EVENT for Women for Afghan Women on November 29 and 30, 2001, was a conference of Afghan women scholars and activists held at the Graduate Center of the City University of New York. The conference traced the history of Afghan women's rights, the rights accorded to women under Islam, the abuses perpetrated by the Taliban, and women's priorities in post-Taliban Afghanistan.

The panels included not only Afghan women engaged in significant aspects of reconstruction such as nation building, public health, and economics, but also Muslim theologians, American feminists, United Nations (UN) representatives, historians, and journalists—non-Afghans who have demonstrated their solidarity with Afghan women in key ways, especially during the Taliban years. Most essays in this book are by panelists at our conference. Some are modified versions of papers delivered at the conference, and others were written specially for this book. Together, they are a dynamic group of essays providing women's reflections and solutions for a world at war. Voices that are often at odds—those for or against secular government in Afghanistan, those who are or are not rooted in Islam, those with varying opinions of the American/Western women's movement and differing definitions of feminism—were brought together at our conference and continue their dialogue within the covers of this book.

Two of the essays are by women who were in Bonn, Germany, during the UN-sponsored meetings that led to the formation of the interim government: Sima Wali, an official delegate, and Rina Amiri, a member of a nongovernmental organization coalition. Their essays serve as bookends to this collection—as foreword and epilogue.

The first section includes essays that chart history in order to seek a way out of war and devastation. The second section offers stories, testimonies, and strategies of diverse Afghan women engaged in the reconstruction of Afghanistan and of non-Afghan women who ensure that America, its women's movement, and the world will not abandon our Afghan sisters and brothers.

Qur'anic scholar Sanaa Nadim and feminist theologian Riffat Hassan implore us to understand that Islam undergirds the lives of most Afghan women. Sister Nadim refers to the Qur'anic texts and notable Muslim women throughout Islamic history to argue that Afghan women need not "alter [their] inherent value system" in order to advocate for their own rights. Riffat Hassan brings our attention to "the vast majority of Afghan women who are struggling to maintain their religious identity and personal autonomy in the face of the intransigence of Muslim culture, on the one hand, and the imperialism of Western, secular culture, on the other hand."

Ten of the essays are by Afghan women. Weeda Mansoor, a member of the Revolutionary Association of the Women of Afghanistan (RAWA), gives a history of abuses against women under the Soviets, under the mujahideen, and finally under the Taliban. Mansoor expresses the rage of an organization that has been on the frontlines of the Afghan women's fight for survival and offers a critique of the process by which Afghanistan is currently being rebuilt. Sara Amiryar educates us about the history of the *loya jirga,* the parliamentary process that Afghan leaders have traditionally reverted to in times of national crisis. Amiryar feels that "the only way that Afghanistan can take the next step into the future is through a globally supported *loya jirga.*" Fahima Vorgetts has been a women's activist since the age of ten, when she was involved in the earliest days of the Women's Democratic Organization in Afghanistan. Vorgetts advocates that the reconstruction of Afghanistan must have among its guiding tenets a gradual community-based approach, a secular governance system, and the prioritization of education for all. Zohra Yusuf Daoud tells her own story about being raised in progressive and affluent Kabul in the 1960s, and becoming the first and, thus far, the only Miss Afghanistan, in 1972. Zohra Rasekh brings a hard-hitting reality check to the collection—her research into the health of Afghan women and her horrifying findings demonstrate that physical and mental healthcare must be a priority as Afghanistan is rebuilt.

Sima Wali, Sara Amiryar, Fahima Vorgetts, and Rina Amiri have become advisory committee members of Women for Afghan Women and mentors to the youngest contributor to the volume—Masuda Sultan. Sultan is an Afghan American activist and community organizer who has taken on a leadership role within Women for Afghan Women. Both she and Fariba Nawa, an Afghan American journalist and writer, describe through personal testimony the existential dilemmas and experiences of being of two worlds and reconciling the American with the Afghan self, especially at a time when the two nations are at war.

Eleanor Smeal, Gloria Steinem, Ruth Messinger, Angela King, Felicity Hill, Mikele Aboitiz, and Irena Lieberman are American women who have been pioneers in their activism and service on behalf of Afghan women. Smeal and Steinem remind us of the importance of learning from the successes and lessons of our past. Messinger gives a resounding rally cry to the courageous women of Afghanistan as they "take their rightful place in their country and change the future." King's essay is a detailed history of the United Nations' support of the Afghan people, especially its women. Hill and Aboitiz educate us about an important resolution that their organization, Women's International League for Peace and Freedom (WILPF), helped secure for the women of the world: Security Resolution 1325. "Women finally have a tool they can use to become part of the planning for the future of their country." Lieberman, a legal representative and advocate for refugees, writes about the overwhelming obstacles confronted by Afghan women seeking asylum in the United States.

Arline Lederman, Elizabeth Gould, and Paul Fitzgerald are Americans who have lived and worked in Afghanistan and have developed not just expertise in the history and culture, but also intimacy with the people of that nation. Lederman provides a history of the role of women in Afghanistan as she has experienced and witnessed it; and Gould and Fitzgerald write about their journalistic efforts in Afghanistan over the past two decades to "solve the riddle" of the global politics of Afghanistan, "caught between the three worlds of religion, modern politics, and the Western dream."

To contextualize the pieces in the book, I have included a photo essay by Italian photographer Lina Pallotta and poetry by Fevziye Rahzogar Barlas, Freshta Amirzada, and Atia Gaheez. At the end of the book, I have provided five appendixes: an informational page about Women for Afghan Women; a bibliography on Afghanistan and Afghan women; a list of organizations and resources addressing Afghan women's rights; and biographical information about the authors.

It is important to note here that the views expressed in each paper are the authors' alone. I have chosen these papers to represent the vast spectrum of opinion among those who are wholeheartedly committed to and active in the struggle for Afghan women's rights. All but one of the Afghan contributors have returned to Afghanistan since September 11, and all are contributing in one way or another to the reconstruction process. Women for Afghan Women has spent its first year acting as a bridge between Afghan women's rights activists living in the United States, Afghan communities in the United States, especially New York, and American feminist and human rights activists. We have learnt that a further bridge must be built and strengthened—between the diverse Afghan women who remained in Afghanistan during its darkest years and have persisted and survived, and those who left Afghanistan as exiles and refugees. Our organization is positioned to bring together the courage, rage, and wisdom of experience of the former with the resources, passion, and heartfelt desire to help of the latter.

May Afghanistan realize that its greatest untapped resource as it seeks a new destiny is *all* its women.

AFGHANISTAN

TRUTH AND MYTHOLOGY

SIMA WALI

EVER SINCE MY RETURN in October 2001 from the Afghan refugee camps in Pakistan, where I listened to the voices of hundreds of increasingly desperate women and men, I have anguished over how to explain what I have learned—that the true needs and wants of the Afghan people are largely absent from campaigns waged on their behalf in the United States. As an Afghan activist who has worked for over twenty years to bring about sustainable change in the living conditions of Afghan women and men, I still grieve for the Afghanistan that has been lost. But what disturbs me more is the new Afghanistan that is emerging to replace it. The failure of the West to influence events in Afghanistan cannot be attributed only to the growth of extremist Islam and tribalism. Rather, it is a direct result of the long-standing inability of Western institutions to adjust to the realities of what needs to be done and to listen to the voices of the vast majority of Afghans, who are capable of ushering in democratic change and are willing to do so.

A narrowness permeates American thinking and appears to render America deaf to the voices and tears of the Afghan people, who have struggled to survive what has come to be seen as an American policy of abandonment. It was to understand their pain and their vision that I left the safety of the United States and embarked on a dangerous mission to Pakistan. But any danger to me was minimal compared with the danger faced by the courageous people who ventured out to meet me. The women of Afghanistan and their male escorts braved mine-fields and dangerous mountain passes to conduct secret meetings with me in a dusty border town in Pakistan where Afghan refugees live under the most primitive conditions. Many women I spoke to were new arrivals who had just crossed the border, fleeing drought and war. They were activists and leaders who, to the best of their ability, tried to provide education, health, and social services to war-affected Afghans both inside Afghanistan and within Pakistan. They were fighters for human rights, fiercely dedicated to a vision of dignity, safety, and freedom for Afghans.

For two weeks I listened to these visionaries, who had been trauma-tized by twenty-three years of war but were still dreaming and strug-gling to make their dreams a reality. They spoke of grinding, devastating poverty, growing numbers of suicides, and a mounting de-spair that their dreams for a free Afghanistan would be swallowed ei-ther by an international army of Islamic mercenaries supplied by Pakistan or by the misguided interventions of the Western world.

My colleagues and I met with representatives from forty-five civic organizations led by Afghan women and men. In total, these organiza-tions represented all segments of the Afghan population, crossing every divide—ethnic, gender, age, and sectarian. Because I am Afghan, they trusted me, often divulging experiences, dreams, nightmares, and hopes they could not easily express to others. The picture that emerged has haunted me every day since my return.

The Afghans I was privileged to meet, and those I did not meet, were hungry and traumatized. They received no health services. They could not learn new skills since they had no access to education or to societal resources. They were forbidden from operating civic institutions. "We are a proud nation but our dignity has been trampled on," they told me desperately again and again.

These are the yet-unheard voices of the grassroots community leaders who against all odds are rebuilding the shattered lives of women, men, the elderly, the handicapped, orphaned children, and land mine victims. Their work receives no support from international relief agencies, and they struggle alone to tend to the needs of Afghans in Pakistan, whose living situation has deteriorated over the past years.

I carry the message not only of leaders but also of ordinary Afghan citizens and youth who ardently sought me out, beseeching me to report on the effect of misguided refugee policies and their callous disregard for human lives.

My Afghan sisters and brothers asked me to "bear witness to our suffering" and "get those of our faith to help us solve our own problems." They were acutely aware of their extreme poverty, seeing themselves as among the poorest of the world's poor and calling themselves "a nation of female beggars." Most tragically, they feel forgotten and betrayed by the world, especially the United States. They feel that they were used as a tool by the United States in the battle against the Soviet Union and were then discarded once American objectives were met. "We fought to bring an end to communism with the help of the United States," one woman told me, "but then America, too, abandoned us." Ultimately, their varied accounts can be summarized by a single plea that was unanimously echoed again and again: "We are looking for you to amplify our voices, which remain silenced to people in the free world."

I am honor-bound to carry their words to Americans in the hope that on every level, from the administration to civilians who "just want to help," policies for involvement with Afghanistan will be aligned with the goals, dreams, and real needs of the Afghan people.

HUMAN RIGHTS ISSUES IN PAKISTAN

Although some attention has been paid to the problems of Afghans in major cities inside Afghanistan, little attention has been given to the estimated 2 million Afghan refugees, the majority of whom are women living in exile in Pakistan. At the time of my visit, these numbers were increasing daily due to drought, famine, war, unavailability of health services, and ongoing gender-based persecution. Although many Afghan-run community associations were based in Pakistan and extended their services to Afghans caught in the war zones inside Afghanistan, only a few such groups had permits to function in Pakistan. The others, which were completely isolated from international donor agency support or the UN system, were harassed and occasionally shut down.

Afghan educators bitterly complained to me of ongoing harassment by Pakistani police. Because these educators are denied the proper registration documents and the authorization to serve their communities, they are regarded as engaging in "illegal activities." Even in those few cases where they have obtained permission, they must contend with host-country bureaucracy that severely hampers their ability to be effective.

And where can these Afghans take their grievances? Nowhere. There is no court of appeal, no authority sympathetic to their needs or concerned about the injustices they were suffering. Most Afghans living in exile in Pakistan are deemed de facto refugees and are not granted official status by the United Nations High Commissioner for Refugees (UNHCR).

The majority of Afghans who had sought asylum felt that the Pakistani town of Peshawar, where a great number had taken refuge, was a microcosm of life under the Taliban. Although there were no official laws in place that actually replicated the brutal and unyielding edicts of the Taliban regime, many human rights abuses were comparable. Afghan culture and traditions were not respected. Women were still required to have male escorts and were subject to discrimination and ill treatment. Children bore the brunt of dislocation, poverty, and the inability to obtain an education. "Our children are forced into child labor," the teachers told me, complaining that "children fall asleep in classes" after arriving in school exhausted from their jobs. Forced to study in a foreign language, Urdu (the official language of Pakistan), with no standard curriculum, Afghan children were gradually becoming indoctrinated to an alien culture.

BEYOND THE GENDER DIVIDE— THE ROLE OF MEN

Since the advent of the Taliban and ensuing edicts against women, Western eyes have rightly focused on Afghan "gender apartheid." But American feminists and the media have been so concerned with the treatment of women that they have ignored the real role of Afghan men. It may surprise Westerners to discover that the stereotype of Afghan men as women-haters and oppressors is incorrect. Most Afghan men are committed to the cause of better conditions and freedom for Afghan women. They have stepped in to provide women-specific education and agricultural training and have been willing to serve as intermediaries in the marketplace, where women still cannot move about freely. The importance of this latter contribution on the part of men cannot be stressed sufficiently. Afghan women–led community-based groups in both countries lack training, information, permits, fax machines, telephones, paid staff, and computers to conduct their services, but most important, Afghan women lack mobility. Men who accompany and assist women in their work are providing an essential service.

The Afghan women I interviewed repeatedly requested that their men be supported to advance the cause of Afghan women. They want these men to be regarded as part of the solution, not part of the problem. I was heartened to witness the passionate defense of Afghan women's leadership and empowerment by Afghan men from various ethnicities. In the West, this vital contribution is not understood.

An example of this Western disregard for the role and needs of men is the effort of the U.S. government to designate funds for the education of Afghan girls in an attempt to rectify the harsh effects of Taliban edicts barring female education. For all its good intentions, the effort is misguided because it has created yet another problem—educational programs that exclude boys. Lack of available education for boys in Afghanistan and in Pakistani refugee camps drove many Afghan families to resort to the only recourse available—the *madressas* in Pakistan. These notorious seminaries are the very same institutions that indoctrinated and educated the Taliban. One male educator passionately defended schooling for young boys as well as girls by saying "If keeping girls from education is tantamount to cutting off one arm, keeping boys from education cuts off the other. We need both arms to function."

AFGHAN MYTHOLOGY

Part of the overwhelming responsibility that has been entrusted to me by the precious people whom I interviewed is to carry not only their pain and suffering but also their triumph to the Western world. The dignity, courage, dedication, and vision I encountered belies the notion that they are only victims. The image of Afghans as miserable victims is but one of a series of myths created and perpetuated by the Western world. I believe that part of the sacred responsibility with which I was charged is to dispel misunderstandings and rectify misconceptions.

For over 200 years, Afghanistan has been the object of Western myth, a land little understood but romanticized by many in Europe and America. That myth was played on following the Soviet invasion of Afghanistan 1979. It took the form of regarding Afghans as fiercely religious freedom fighters, and it won hearts and minds to the Afghan cause. During those terrible years, Afghans built many myths about the West as well. We believed that once our country was freed from the tyranny and slavery of an invading nation, we—men and women—

could rebuild the land and share in a great freedom by building on the foundation of democracy.

Our disillusionment and the dispelling of our myth regarding the United States began long before Americans were forced to reexamine their own myths. For us, the callous abandonment of Afghan needs by the United States following the successful campaign against the Soviet Union took place over a decade ago. We were forced to look at the true nature of our "allies" and acknowledge the harsh reality that we were now left to our own devices by an opportunistic government. But Americans were allowed to hold on to their myths about us, a vision that included some combination of belief in our fierceness and pity for our victimization. All of the myths surrounding us were ultimately informed by the most insidious myth of all—that the plight of Afghans has no relevance to the rest of the world, that Afghans do not need to be understood and their needs do not have to be met.

It is unfortunate that it took an act of war against the American people to focus attention on the long-standing humanitarian and political crisis in Afghanistan. For too long Afghanistan has been viewed as irrelevant, to the detriment of innocent Americans and those in the larger world community. The glaring human rights abuses in Afghanistan were allowed to continue with international impunity until the crimes extended their reach to residents of the United States. Through the tragic events of September 11, Americans painfully learned that what happens in Kabul directly affects people all over the world.

Over the years, I have struggled to convey the horror endured by my people, especially the women, without much success. I have pleaded on behalf of the voices of the Afghan people, shattered and silenced for twenty-three years. I have striven to bring to Western public attention the perspectives of the vast majority of moderate-minded Afghans. My message fell on unreceptive ears. Now perhaps there is hope.

The ferocity of the terrorist attacks of September 11 initially put Afghanistan and its dignified people, most of whom crave peace, in the worst possible and most unsympathetic light at a time when they desperately needed the support of the international community. However, as the situation began to unfold in all its horror and complexity during the days and weeks following the attack, it became increasingly clear that this horrendous event brought unexpected opportunity for a major transformation in Afghanistan. Ironically, an unintended consequence of September 11 is that new light has been shed on the country. It is to be hoped that this light will illuminate new pathways of freedom, autonomy, and democracy for Afghanistan. After having been ignored for more than two decades, Afghanistan is once again at the forefront of the political arena. For the first time in many years there is fluidity, movement, and possibility in the country. This is an unprecedented and historic moment, a window of opportunity to enact the goals and implement the vision toward which I have been working for so long.

A major shift in policy is the only solution to the dire problems of the roughly estimated 24 million Afghan people, of which, according to the latest Central Intelligence Agency estimates, 12 million are women. But in order for this to happen, the West must listen to authentic Afghan voices.

THE TRUE NATURE OF THE AFGHAN PEOPLE

Listening to the voices of Afghans begins with understanding who they are—and who they are not. Earlier I referred to myths and stereotypes that have informed Western policy toward Afghanistan. I would like to lay out in greater detail some basic facts about Afghanistan and the Afghan people and to dispel some glaring misconceptions.

- The people of Afghanistan are called Afghans, not Afghanis. An Afghani is a unit of money.
- Afghans are not Arabs, nor are they of Middle Eastern or Persian origin.

- Afghans speak Dari, not Arabic or Persian. Although Dari resembles the language spoken in modern-day Iran, it is also quite different. [Editor's note: Pashto is also widely spoken.]
- The Afghan people have not been the enemy of the West. The Afghans were aligned with the United States and lost 2 million lives fighting with the United States to bring down communism.
- While most Afghans are Muslim, this does not mean that they are militant Islamic fundamentalists. The vast majority of Afghans are moderate thinking and peace-loving. Islam is a peace-loving and tolerant religion that does not include compulsion. Fanatics from Saudi Arabia, Pakistan, and elsewhere have imposed extremist forms of Islam, such as Deobandi and Wahabi, on the Afghan people.
- The majority of those defined as terrorists, including those who committed the heinous acts of September 11, are not of Afghan descent. Most are of Middle Eastern, Pakistani, and North African origin.
- Afghans in the United States are not aligned with terrorists. On the contrary, many fled the same oppressors who have harbored and supported the terrorists who attacked the United States. The Afghans remaining in their home country have themselves been held hostage by the Taliban militia and its Pakistani and Arab supporters. Afghans have come forward to condemn the terrorist attacks waged in the name of Islam. It is a travesty of justice and a perversion of truth to regard the Afghan people as the enemy.
- The Taliban were not elected by the Afghan people and were never regarded by the population as the legitimate government of Afghanistan. On the contrary, Afghans viewed, and continue to view, the Taliban as an invading force created and supported by Pakistani intelligence services and its Arab allies. Osama bin Laden was *not* an invited guest of the Afghan people.
- The estimated 50,000 to 80,000 Pakistani, Arab, and other foreign mercenaries in Afghanistan have wreaked untold havoc on the Afghan people. Their agenda has been to destroy Afghan

culture, identity, and psyche and to impose their own extremist policies to serve their own agenda. The Soviet Union used similar tactics when it invaded Afghanistan. The destruction of Afghan's pre-Islamic heritage, including the ancient statuary of the famous Buddhas, the imposition of Arabic and Urdu, and the extreme practices of gender apartheid are unprecedented in Afghan history and culture. The Afghan people have been terrorized by these foreign forces. They do not support them.

SUSTAINABLE SOLUTIONS FOR THE FUTURE

Solutions can be born only from an understanding of the problem. I began by laying out the conditions of Afghan refugees and continued by dispelling myths and explaining who the Afghans are. Now we can examine specific strategies that address the needs of the Afghan people. I would again like to emphasize that these strategies cannot be externally imposed. They must arise from the self-understanding of the people whom they affect.

The neglect of male secular education described earlier is one example of the Western tendency to impose someone else's agenda on Afghan people without full understanding or regard for the real needs demanded by the situation. Solutions like these create more problems than they resolve and do not meet the needs of the people they are trying to help.

In December 2001 I served as an official delegate in the UN Peace Talks on Afghanistan in Bonn. I represented the former King of Afghanistan, his Majesty Mohammad Zahir Shah. I also was the main organizer for the Afghan Women's Summit for Democracy held in Brussels in late 2001. These contexts, coupled with my personal visits to Pakistan, have enabled me to lay out a list of six priorities of the Afghan people themselves.

1. *Reconstruction assistance to Afghanistan that furthers the end of long-term development is top priority.* Even emergency humanitar-

ian aid, though vitally important, neglects the development of community-based civic leadership. It provides only temporary, short-term solutions to permanent problems and ignores the people necessary to rebuild society. The fundamental problems facing Afghans will not be resolved by the importing of food and medical assistance from outside. Solutions, which can come only from within the Afghan community itself, must focus not only on the physical needs of the people—food, shelter, medical care—but also on the long-term goal of creating a tolerant, civil, and democratic Afghan society such as existed during the democracy-building era prior to the Soviet invasion in 1979, a time when women were active in political and non-political spheres. Innovative approaches, such as the empowerment of Afghan civic leaders from across ethnic, sectarian, and gender divides, are essential precursors for the development of this type of society.

Afghans seek to be linked to democratic-minded and civic institutions in the free world. But they need technical assistance and access to information technology to implement exchange programs with the West. Rapid and long-term development projects aimed at strengthening Afghan community-based institutions through direct financial aid are priorities consistently identified by the Afghan people.

The work of the United States Agency for International Development (USAID) to provide development assistance in support of reconstruction and democracy building is hampered by a lack of government-appropriated long-term funds. It is critical to provide indigenous nongovernmental organizations, particularly those that are women-led, with long-term aid to create sustainable civil-society structures.

2. *Sustained international pressure on members of the interim government to ensure that women play a prominent role in the post-Taliban government.* As one of the three women delegates to the

Bonn peace talks, I strongly advocated for the creation of the Ministry of Women's Affairs and the nomination of Dr. Sima Samar as one of the vice chairs of the interim government. It is my firm belief that there is a need to create political space for more Afghan women to take active roles in governing Afghanistan now that all factions have signed a peace agreement.

Prior to participating in the UN Peace Talks on Afghanistan, I was instrumental in securing unprecedented written and verbal statements from former President Burhanuddin Rabbani, former King Mohammad Zahir Shah, and the current interim Interior Minister, Yunus Kanouni, supporting the role of Afghan women in high-level government positions. These historic statements concretize the king's often-forgotten stance on the role of women in Afghan society; during his reign we saw the establishment of the first coeducational Afghan university in 1947 and women's faculty in 1948, and the installation of the 1964 Constitution granting equal rights to women. We now need to ensure that these promises are converted to real action. I am heartened that Afghan women have been included in this initial phase of the new political process, and I hope that this positive trend will continue into the future.

3. Now that Afghanistan has been accorded center stage in the war against terrorism, *it is incumbent on every nation to initiate a partnership among democratic-minded Afghan citizens to eradicate all forms of terrorism, particularly violence against Afghan women.* The Afghan people must be included in developing a sustainable and comprehensive response to root out terrorism rather than a meaningless, Band-Aid solution. An open society in which people are empowered is the best insurance against terrorism.

4. *Afghan youth—boys as well as girls—must be provided with vocational education and adult literacy as well as formal education.* They need to learn practical skills and to master the academic disciplines that will enable them to interact with the world out-

side their own country. Boys need secular educational institutions so that they are not thrust into the portals of the *madressas*.

5. *The abject poverty that has plagued the Afghan nation must be addressed with short-term humanitarian assistance and, more important, with long-term financial commitment to grassroots organizations that will enact the most lasting changes.*

6. *Powerful state institutions must be balanced by people's and civil institutions.* We Afghans need the backing of the international community and the United Nations to ensure that this time around there is "staying power" on the part of the United States, coupled with a serious effort to resolve the deep-rooted crisis.

CONCLUSION

I am proud to be an Afghan, a Muslim, a woman, and an American. I will not be forced into becoming an apologist for any of these identities. My culture does not dehumanize women. My religion does not promote the bondage of women. It does not advocate the rape, pillage, or imprisonment of women. It does not drive them into poverty or starvation, deny them education or medical care, and countenance torture. It saddens me to see the valiant people of Afghanistan depicted as perpetrators of heinous crimes while it is they who are the victims. The real perpetrators have betrayed Afghan culture and religion by invoking them as justification for their non-Islamic and non-Afghan acts of brutality. The world can no longer claim ignorance while witnessing atrocities carried out against Afghan women, children, and men in the name of saving them. Afghans need freedom-loving women and men from around the world to rise up on their behalf to demand the intervention of a global coalition to bring peace, not relentless bombing and continued war.

We must stay true to the pledge the world made at the United Nations Genocide Convention in 1948 in Paris that "never again" would an entire people be systematically destroyed. The Afghan people feel that humanity has broken that promise, has permitted atrocities to be committed against them. May this juncture of history bring a lasting peace. *Never again* may the Afghan people be subjected to horror and cruelty.

BUILDING COMMUNITY ACROSS DIFFERENCE

Sunita Mehta and Homaira Mamoor

AS WE WRITE THIS INTRODUCTION, Ahmedabad, in Sunita's country, India, is ablaze. Hindus are burning Muslims alive and torching their property—this in response to Muslims setting on fire a train full of Hindus. This same week, as we huddle over a laptop computer in Brooklyn, Hamid Karzai, interim prime minister of Homaira's Afghanistan, is visiting India and sprinkling rose petals on Mohandas K. Gandhi's memorial. According to Karzai, Gandhi was the apostle of peace and Afghanistan is a country in need of peace today.[1] Homaira has been leafing through the Hindu text that guided Gandhi's nonviolent resistance to the British, the *Bhagavad Gita*, as Sunita looks through the Qur'an to find references to women's rights. We are a Hindu Indian and a Muslim Afghan, two women banding together not only to work for Afghan women, who have been so harshly treated by history, but to challenge the extremists within both our faiths by the simple act of working together. Because both of our faiths, we believe, are animated by the same ideals: peace and justice.

SUNITA

I was born in Madras, India, in 1968, and I grew up in India and England in a modern and devout Hindu family. I consider myself fortunate to have many wonderful role models—women in my family who are leaders in their professions, while also being the bedrock of their homes.

I moved to New York in 1988, to marry, finish college, and start my career. My formal higher education is in mathematics and sociology, and I have spent my entire working life in various women's organizations, all working toward gender equality. The Sister Fund, a feminist women's foundation, has been my professional home for many years. Here I honed the skill of supporting and embracing other women's struggles without owning them. The Sister Fund affords me a broad vantage point over the global women's movement.

I consider myself to be a women's rights activist as well as a South Asian community activist. I have worked as a volunteer and board member of SAKHI for South Asian Women for close to a decade. SAKHI, which means "woman friend" in most South Asian languages and serves women from all South Asian countries (but primarily Hindu and Muslim women from India, Pakistan, and Bangladesh), investigates and confronts domestic abuse in New York's South Asian community. I'm not satisfied to hover at the margins of a social problem, merely peering in and voicing dissent. Rather, I work where most women live, *within* the community, exposing injustices and working to change them.

During the late 1990s, I became aware of the egregiously cruel treatment of Afghan women under the Taliban. The geographic and cultural proximity of Afghanistan to India made the issue particularly personal and urgent for me, and I felt an intense calling to become involved in the struggle of Afghan women. Although I supported the existing efforts in the women's movement, including the work of the Feminist Majority Foundation, I yearned to know the feelings of Afghan women here in the United States. Then Charlotte Bunch, the director of the Center for Women's Global Leadership, a women's human rights organization based at Rutgers University in New Jersey, pointed out to me that any effort to address Afghan women's rights must be spearheaded by Afghan women or it would not be regarded as authentic.

So I began to search for Afghan women activists in New York. When I met a young and spirited Afghan activist, Fahima Danishgar, in early spring 2001 at an introductory lunch meeting at the Zen Palate Restaurant in lower Manhattan, my first question was "What do the women in your community say about the Taliban?" And so began the conversation that led to the founding of Women for Afghan Women (WAW) a full five months before the Twin Towers were razed. By the time New York City was attacked, we had already established a community outreach program designed to assess the priorities of Afghan women in New York. We had also created the structure, speaker wish list, and themes of our conference.

On September 11, when I saw the black cloud in the sky above my son's school in Brooklyn and the images of the planes crashing into the World Trade Center, and then when I learned about Al Qaeda, I had to conclude that this terrible act was a desecration of Islam. I had come to know many more Muslim women by then. For many of them feminist struggle goes hand in hand with their Muslim identity, their faith, and their cultural pride. I respect the peaceful vision of my new Muslim friends—women who are secure in their religion and do not believe in religious coercion or support terrorist activities. Religious historian Karen Armstrong summarized my own feelings when she wrote "the terrorists and their extremist cohorts hijacked not only several planes but one of the world's greatest religions as well."[2]

HOMAIRA

I was born in Kabul, Afghanistan, in 1968. I grew up in a loving family with parents, brothers, aunts and uncles, lots of cousins, and my grandmother in one big house, which was a typical way of life in Afghanistan. My family was in the money exchange and import-export business, and we lived in Kartay Say, a community of upper-class Afghan families and foreign diplomats. I attended a coed school through the sixth grade, studying the Qur'an, math, English, social studies, and science. We also had a summer house in Paghman, a beautiful resort city a hundred miles outside Kabul. A river flowed behind the house and mountains rose spectacularly in the distance. I was devastated when I saw this paradise in ruins in Saira Shah's documentary *Beneath the Veil* on CNN.

My father would not live in a country that denied its citizens basic human rights and freedom. Besides, he despised the Communists! So after the first coup in 1978, my family moved to the United States. The most tragic part of the migration was leaving behind my beloved grandmother, but we all thought the separation would be brief. My father always dreamed of going back, but he died in 1985 when he was forty-two years old. Then my older brother had to drop out of college and become the family breadwinner.

We moved on with our lives—I went to college, married, became the mother of three girls—but we have always loved our homeland. We talked all the time, at home and in the mosque, about the terrible treatment of women and children by the Taliban. The stories of unlucky families, of mothers and sisters trapped inside that forsaken country, broke our hearts. But what was most heartwrenching was the way these crimes were perpetrated in the name of my peaceful religion. What the Taliban were preaching and practicing was an affront and an embarrassment to Islam in particular and humanity in general.

The religion I know respects women. As far back as the seventh century, it freed them from oppressive conditions in the Arabian peninsula and elevated their status. Muslim women could keep their own names after marriage, they could earn and keep their own money, and they could divorce. Islam gave women financial independence and equality with men in all acts of piety at a time when the rest of the world gave women no such rights.

When I saw the three young Uzbek sisters in *Beneath the Veil* who were probably raped and who were forced to watch their mother being shot, I was moved to tears. But I could cry only so much. And after September 11, I had to do more than donate money and sign petitions. It was time for action. That was when I joined Women for Afghan Women (WAW) and vowed to fight until Afghan women are freed from oppression.

Now I can and will do more than just cry.

I'm committed to empowering my Afghan sisters through education. If we're going to reach Muslim women, we must do it through education and through their religion. The Muslim women I know are devout. They attend the mosque, they recite the Qur'an, and they listen to the imam when he preaches. But because most of them have memorized the Qur'an in Arabic, a language they don't speak or understand, or because they read translations of it written by men, they don't know what rights they have under Islam. Many believe that reciting verses by rote is all that's required of them. Some of them have an idea that these rights exist, but they don't know how to claim them. They don't know that men who oppress women in the name of Islam are really ignorant when it comes to the religion. They don't understand the difference between religion on the one hand and culture and custom on the other.

Afghan women have been through so much emotional and psychological stress that it's difficult to reach them. This is the challenge for us: how to reach the minds and hearts of these women, who have been deprived of the true meaning of their faith. How do we talk to them? When they refuse to come to us, how do we get them out of their houses and then out of the dark? I believe I've done a service if I can teach my own three girls their rights and religious obligations and if they in turn teach the next generation. If one Muslim woman or girl is moved in some way by our message, we've accomplished something. But I believe we can and will do more. As Sunita has said, "We are activists for justice," and the noble intent of the Qur'an is justice.

THE ROLE OF WAW FOLLOWING SEPTEMBER 11

Women for Afghan Women cosponsored the earliest Muslim peace rallies and teach-ins in New York after the September terrorist attack. While we were tormented by the jingoism and warmongering pervading the media, we could not adopt the unrealistic pacifism of the American peace movement. We knew the urgency of Afghanistan's liberation from terrorist rule, and we asked *how* peace might come about without forceful intervention. If invasion proved necessary, we advocated against a unilateral U.S. force and in favor of a global coalition under UN auspices, a coalition that would remain in Afghanistan until peace and economic stability returned.

It was an ironic moment of personal identity politics for us. We had never been more acutely conscious of being immigrants; and yet we had never felt more like New Yorkers, like Americans. Terrorists thought they were attacking America, and indeed they were—except that the victims of 9/11 hailed from all corners of the world. Something terrible had happened to our home, our beloved New York, and at the same time a bloody retaliation was inevitable against Afghanistan because Osama bin Laden was being harbored there. We were "us" and we were "them" at the same time. And of course, as it turned out, the United States did retaliate: "We" dropped food and bombs on "us," the innocent men, women, and children of Afghanistan.

CAUTIOUS OPTIMISM FOR A NEW AFGHANISTAN

On November 29 and 30, 2001, WAW held a conference at the Graduate Center of the City University of New York, entitled "Women for

Afghan Women: Securing Our Future." It was the first Afghan women's conference ever held in New York. The panels traced the history of women's rights in Afghanistan, addressed the human rights abuses under the Taliban regime and the resulting humanitarian crisis, and charted specific steps to be taken to ensure a just rebuilding of the country, respectful of the human rights of all its people.

Our conference coincided with the historic meetings in Bonn, Germany (November 27–December 6, 2001) that led to the formation of the interim government of Afghanistan. Sima Wali, who was originally our keynote speaker and whose address is included as our foreword, was the first of only three Afghan women invited to participate as delegates in these UN-sponsored meetings. Women hold only two key positions in the new government: Sima Samar is the minister of women's affairs and deputy prime minister, and Suhaila Seddiqi heads the interim Department of Public Health. As in Bonn, women are certainly underrepresented. After all, women make up more than half of the population of Afghanistan.

On January 28, 2002, members of WAW attended an event introducing interim prime minister Hamid Karzai to the local Afghan community at the Grand Hyatt Hotel in New York. We sat behind a group of young Afghan children, who were dressed in ethnic clothes and were ready to welcome the prime minister. The children streamed to the stage and honored Mr. Karzai. As they returned, one of them, a girl, found that her front-row seat had been taken by a boy originally in the second row. She looked at him and said forcefully, "No." We asked the boy to return to his original seat, but he simply grinned, knowing even at his early age the privileges of his gender. The little girl sat down near us, annoyed beneath her green shimmering head covering.

But the prime minister's heartfelt and optimistic message, inviting the Afghan diaspora "back home" to be a part of reconstruction, uplifted us. We shared the community's optimism, but it was laced with a chilling realization that the odds were steeply stacked against him. When the audience was invited to write down questions, we addressed ours to Deputy Prime Minister Samar, who was seated on the stage but had not spoken. We also asked the little girl if she had a question for the prime minister. She asked us to write, "My name is Hosni Noorzi, and I am nine years old. When I grow up, I want to be a doctor. When can I return and cure everybody?"

Neither our question nor Hosni's was answered. The prime minister and his colleagues left abruptly. We had experienced the hope of the entire community, and yet we were saddened that so few women had come; that Sima Samar hadn't spoken, indeed hadn't even looked over as we spontaneously chanted "Sima Jan, welcome"; and especially that little Hosni's question was left unanswered.

In Afghanistan itself, girls are beginning to attend school and women's magazines are starting up, but brothels are proliferating, poverty has led some families to sell their children, and widows continue to beg on the streets in order to provide for their children. And there is pervasive warlordism and rape.

It seems clear that women's issues are not at the forefront of the new government's priorities and that only token acknowledgment is being paid to women—possibly to placate the Western world. Possibly some members of the government mistakenly believe that women's issues are less important than other objectives, such as national security and humanitarian aid. This would not be the first time that this set of priorities has been invoked. In 1994 Fatima Gailani—the only woman in the guerrilla army of the Afghan Resistance against the Soviets—disagreed with her father's perspectives regarding women. Her father, Pir Sayed Ahmad Gailani, was the founder of the National Islamic Front of Afghanistan and religious leader of many Sunni Muslims in the country. Though a modern and liberal leader, he believed that women's suffrage should be addressed only after national stability was attained. Fatima disagreed, saying, "I know this will not happen because if you take a first step that is wrong, the rest of the way will be crooked."[3]

These words remain true today and are the core principle of WAW. While we are cognizant of the aspirations of the entire country of Afghanistan for basic goals such as national stability, we maintain that women must be part of every aspect of that stability. Women must play a role in rebuilding every facet of that society. The huge struggle over an entire nation's priorities and its destiny was reflected in our experience of a single boy's disregard for his sister's rights. We know that in the large and the miniature realms, in the public and the private domains, the struggle of Afghan women continues.

THE CORNERSTONES OF WAW

It has been nine tumultuous months since WAW was founded, and we have established the cornerstones of our work: diversity, community, commitment to a just reconstruction, and, of course, to peace and justice for women.

DIVERSITY

WAW is a nonpolitical organization. The ethics that guide and unify us are those of human rights for all and equal and full participation of all women. Our platform can include all Afghans, all people. We have a single faith—a deep faith in the human capacity for justice and human rights.

Our luxury, our privilege, is that we are free, and, despite our concern that Afghan women are still not receiving priority treatment, we have our optimism intact. The solution to the problem of Afghanistan lies in the banding together of its different ethnic and political factions for the sake of their nation and their people. WAW is a diverse group, with women of many faiths, nationalities, and ideologies; the Afghan members themselves are diverse in ethnicity and background. If *we* can work together, addressing and overcoming our differences, united in our efforts to empower Afghan women, perhaps we can serve as a model for the way forward.

COMMUNITY

The constituency that we serve and empower are Afghan women in Afghanistan and New York City, who live in communities and families and work within and outside the home. Ninety-nine percent of Afghans are Muslim.[4] The most effective way of reaching them is to speak from the standpoint of their own religious and national history, which accords them rights and equality. In fact, "the emancipation of women was a project dear to the Prophet's heart. The Qur'an gave women rights of inheritance and divorce long before Western women were accorded such status."[5] As early as 1921, King Amanollah Shah abolished the mandatory donning of the *burqa,* and his wife, Queen Soraya, appeared in public unveiled and wearing skirts that revealed her legs. Afghanistan's 1964 constitution guaranteed equality and the vote for women; in fact, women participated in the drafting of that constitution. Immediately before the Taliban took power, women in Kabul did not wear *burqas.* Seventy percent of schoolteachers, 50 percent of civilian government workers, and 40 percent of healthcare workers were female. At Kabul University, more than 50 percent of students and 60 percent of teachers were women.[6]

WAW members who hail from Afghanistan but not from Kabul remind us that not all of Afghanistan was a part of the liberalization process that took place in the last century. Rural Afghanistan—especially Pashtun Afghanistan—is, and has been, tremendously patriarchal. WAW hopes to prioritize reconstruction projects in the most conservative parts of the country.

Tamim Ansary, an Afghan writer and poet who is concerned that the world's attention on Afghan women's status is too narrowly focused on the elite, cautions that:

> The Taliban did not spring directly from hell. They sprang from Afghan culture strained through hell. . . . Wherever Afghans choose their tradi-

tional way of life . . . the international community should work with rather than against the grain of the culture. Empowering women through their traditional roles may lead to the deepest changes. To me, right now, a historic opportunity exists to support the real empowerment of Afghan women without engaging in a cultural tug of war with traditional Afghanistan.[7]

We agree with Mr. Ansary, but only up to a point. Our tug-of-war is with extremism rather than with tradition. The empowerment of Afghan women will be possible through their traditions, provided that the traditions themselves are just. Our commitment to community does not forgive injustice within community. It is high time that Muslims reclaim their religion from the hands of extremists, who know only war and hatred and who have no respect for people's dignity and fundamental human rights. It has been said that "the position of women in Muslim society mirrors the destiny of Islam: when Islam is secure and confident so are its women; when Islam is threatened and under pressure, so, too, are they."[8]

A JUST RECONSTRUCTION

WAW is eager to support the reconstruction efforts, but we realize that the situation in Afghanistan is fragile and uncertain. We therefore hold the world accountable to its promise to help the Afghan people attain peace and stability. We implore the world to:

- Help Afghanistan attain a basic level of security, which is essential for any reconstruction to take place.
- Give aid and monitor all aid to ensure that the money is spent on projects that foster and promote the empowerment of women.
- Support traditional Afghan democratic processes such as the *loya jirga* (representative council of leaders), through which the Afghan people can choose their own leaders.

WOMEN

American feminist Eleanor Smeal of the Feminist Majority Foundation, activist Mavis Leno, and Senator Hillary Rodham Clinton were pioneers in bringing to global attention the plight of Afghan women under the Taliban as early as 1997. Their efforts succeeded in changing U.S policy "from unconditionally accepting the Taliban to unconditionally rejecting them."[9]

Now it is time for Afghan women to take agency, confident in the support of the world. WAW's greatest aspiration is to enable this to happen. Afghan women will never again be alone because their cause is just. We will not cease our efforts until the day that Afghan women reclaim their right to dignity, self-determination, a life without violence, and full participation in society.

NOTES

1. "New Delhi gives $10mn grant to Afghanistan." *Gulf Times,* Qatar, February 28, 2002.
2. Karen Armstrong, "Was It Inevitable? Islam Through History, " in *How Did This Happen? Terrorism and the New War,* ed. J. Hoge and G. Rose (New York: Public Affairs, 2001), p. 70.
3. Quoted in Jan Goodwin, *Price of Honor: Muslim Women Lift the Veil of Silence on the Islamic World* (New York: Dutton/Plume, 1995), p. 84.
4. Jim Garamone, "Afghanistan: A Battleground Through the Ages," American Forces Press Service, September 19, 2001.
5. Karen Armstrong, *Islam* (New York: Modern Library, Random House, 2000), p. 16.
6. Foreign Policy in Focus, www.fpif.org/faq/0111afghwomen_body.html.
7. Tamim Ansary, "Leaping to Conclusions," *Salon.com,* December 17, 2000.
8. Ahmed Akbar, quoted in Goodwin, *Price of Honor,* p. 47.
9. Ahmed Rashid, *Taliban: Militant Islam, Oil and Fundamentalism in Central Asia* (New Haven, CT: Yale University Press, 2000), p. 182.

Section One

The Lessons of History

Women Have No Name in That Land

FEVZIYE RAHZOGAR BARLAS

Oh dear woman!
I can see you
Sitting with your broken wings

I can see you
Burying your rebellion
In the hurting corner of your cage

I can see you
Residing in the city of darkness
A city without light

In the shade of the land of grief
Where all are departing
You see the flight of your nation
Dawn and sundown
Towards other lands

You, the mother of green fantasies
You, the frightened witness of endless deaths and revenge
I can see you

I can see you
Cursing the terror of war

Your tender smile
Is rusted
In the blurred reflection of the mirror of time

Your silent eyes
In the dancing figures of the shadows
Which are the messengers of the night
Are waiting to salute the arrival of the light

Oh you, the uncomplaining mother of sorrows
You, the silent bird of the burned nests
Your name
Is a ghost
In the realm of horror and death

Your dreams
Are all
In the custody of pain and torment
Don't you know?
Women have no name in that land
                              —translated from Persian by the author

Afghan Women

An Allegory

FRESHTA AMIRZADA

Women pass quietly
in the cities of Afghanistan
camouflaged in long veiled dresses
women once known with reverence and honor
for being teachers, professors, doctors and nurses
women who once adorned the streets with style
with perfect features composed with colors
a noble life now held hostage
women invisible and unknown
raped of status and rights
they walk through the endless days
dominated with calamity.

Behind sealed doors
every women places a wreath of roses
upon sisters, mothers, or a child's head,
provide each other with fake saffron jewelry
and chant sonorous tunes.

Behind every veiled face
an allegory of experience known

like the thousand spears
pierced upon their bodies
they continue to rise
they continue to provide
a remedy
that will relive within every person
the oath of warmth and compassion
they will awaken every soul
to love, to learn, and to master knowledge
that will liberate them.

Aging Afghanistan
withered roses
cobwebs inside walled homes
a candle continues
and so does the spirit
of women who go on marking life
through writing
through letters
through messages
and by others' whispers
her allegory becomes a legend
forever heard and forever learned.

LOOKING BACK, LOOKING FORWARD

ELEANOR SMEAL

THE FEMINIST MAJORITY FOUNDATION's ongoing Campaign to Stop Gender Apartheid in Afghanistan, which began in 1987, has taught us many valuable lessons about the role of the women's movement in global affairs. First, women's voices will be heard in international relations if we are organized and persistent. When we began our campaign, we were told that we would not be able to organize a grassroots movement on an issue involving women in a remote land so far away. The argument was that the public simply did not care. We proved that women do care, that they can be mobilized, and that indeed they *must* be mobilized. Our campaign generated more mail and e-mail to the U.S. State Department and Clinton administration than any other foreign policy issue during this period and I believe in large measure resulted in the change of U.S. foreign policy to nonrecognition of the Taliban.

Moreover, despite our failure to receive news coverage from the major media, we were able to reach the public with our message through the use of celebrities and the entertainment media, which actually reach more people than the traditional news sources. Most important, we learned that the treatment of women by a government or a regime cannot be ignored. Too often women are the canaries in the coal mine. The women's movement must take itself more seriously and develop a gender perspective on global affairs.

In organizing this campaign, we also learned the strength of the global women's movement. As we organized in the United States, women in Europe, Afghan women's organizations both here and abroad, and women's nongovernmental organizations (NGOs) working with the United Nations (UN) throughout the world organized on behalf of Afghan women. In fact, feminists in high positions in the UN agencies made a significant difference in ensuring that the United Nations would not recognize the Taliban. Together, the global women's movement had a profound impact on ending gender apartheid.

This campaign taught us how small the world really is and that cultural and religious excuses for the abuse and exploitation of people are just a cover. Every time we hear a cultural or a religious justification for inhumane treatment, we must also look at the economic and geopolitical underpinnings of this abuse. To understand Afghanistan and the rise of the Taliban, one must understand the larger context of the major powers' struggle to control the flow of oil and natural resources and the vast amounts of money to be made in the trafficking of drugs, goods, and people.

The tragic lesson of Afghanistan was that ignoring these problems resulted in death and destruction not only within that country and the surrounding areas but also within our own borders. Those of us concerned with feminism must think and act both locally and globally.

To be more specific, our campaign, which involves 205 cosponsoring organizations and 1,065 local action teams throughout the United States, helped bring the Taliban's atrocities against women and girls to the attention of the world and achieved significant changes in U.S. policy toward Afghanistan long before September 11. Chaired by Mavis

Leno, our campaign and the collective efforts of these organizations helped prevent official recognition of the Taliban by the U.S. government and United Nations, increased humanitarian assistance to women and children in Afghanistan and those living as refugees in Pakistan, and stopped construction of an oil pipeline that would have produced over $100 million in royalties for the Taliban.

With the collapse of the Taliban, the advocacy of the U.S. women's movement, along with that of many Afghan women's groups, was instrumental in winning a U.S. commitment to urge that Afghan women be included in leadership roles at every stage of reconstruction. Ultimately, three women delegates were included in the UN-sponsored Bonn negotiations to form an Afghan interim government. Other victories occurred when delegates in the negotiations agreed to the creation of a Ministry for Women's Affairs, which was proposed by Delegate Sima Wali, and the appointments of Dr. Sima Samar, a leading women's rights advocate, as deputy prime minister for women's affairs and General Suhaila Seddiqi, a renowned Kabul surgeon, as minister for public health.

Finally, Afghan women and girls have hope. But the leadership, vigilance, and intensive and continued involvement of the U.S. women's movement and the global women's movement are necessary to make sure that this opportunity is not lost. We must work to ensure that women's rights are fully restored, that women are not marginalized in post-Taliban Afghanistan, that the Afghan Ministry for Women's Affairs receives sufficient funding, that women are represented in all levels of the government of Afghanistan, that U.S. funding for reconstruction is substantial and long term, that peace and security are maintained, and that the many Afghan women-led NGOs that are providing essential health, education, and other services on the ground receive substantial financial support. These are the ingredients necessary for Afghan women and girls to regain their rights and their lives. The writers in this section journey back though time to identify these necessary ingredients—and each proposes her own—for peace and justice in Afghanistan.

WOMEN AND EQUALITY IN ISLAM

SANAA NADIM

AL ISLAM IS THE FAITH of over 1.3 billion people in the world. It is not just a set of dogmas but a living, vibrant way of life. Its message is implied in the many meanings of the word "Islam"—such as "peace" and "surrender to God's will."

What is God's will? Indeed, who is God? According to Islam, God (Allah) is the Creator and the one Supreme Being. He is neither male nor female, nor is He a pluralistic Entity. Rather, He is one, whole and complete, and there is none like Him. Our religion teaches that Allah created humankind and gifted us with prophets to teach and inspire us. Adam is considered a prophet, as are Noah, Abraham, Moses, and Jesus. All were exceptional men who were chosen to appear at different times in history to guide humankind to higher spiritual dimensions by providing them with revelations from God.

The last Prophet and Messenger was Muhammad, Peace be upon Him (PBH). He was born in A.D. 570 in the city of Mecca in Arabia. Our religion teaches that Muhammad received the revelation of the Message of Islam through the holy book of Muslims—the Qur'an. This was revealed to Him when He was forty years old by Archangel Gabriel in the cave of Hira (a cave on the outskirts of Mecca) about 1,436 years ago. The message confirms the validity and authenticity of earlier prophets but goes beyond those teachings and transcends them, offering a new opportunity to unite humanity under the Wings of Mercy.

Muslims refer to the Prophet Muhammad (PBH) in reverential terms because He is considered to be the ultimate teacher and the consummation of all divine contact with humankind. Therefore, pious Muslims usually append the phrase "Peace be upon Him" after invoking His name. I follow in this tradition when I speak and when I write.

The laws of an Islamic state are based on the *Shariya* (the divine law), which derives its rulings from the holy Qur'an and the *Sunnah*— the oral and written teachings about the life of the Prophet Muhammad (PBH).

Having laid out the foundations of Islamic faith, I can turn our attention to the attitude of Islam to women.

The realities that we have seen in recent history regarding the status of women in so-called Muslim countries do not reflect authentic Islam. The Qur'an teaches that religious authorities should generally be obeyed but only if they are carrying out the authentic will of Allah and His Messenger (PBH). However, if you disagree with the authorities of your society or generation because you believe they do not accurately represent the true spirit of Islam, you must go back to the Holy Book and to the *Sunnah* to discern the true message. Human interpretation is neither immutable nor infallible. Therefore, cultural interpretation of Islam is not authentic or binding and, on the contrary, must be overturned by true Muslims if it does not conform to Islamic values.

At no time has this concept been more applicable than today. Extremist Muslims—the West shudders at the phrase—have given all sincere Muslims a bad name. Now *all* Muslims are regarded as "militant fundamentalists," and Islam is seen—incorrectly—as a religion that preaches war rather than peace and advocates oppression of women. The only way to overturn this mistaken concept is to take a careful look at the actual teachings of the Holy Book and at how Islam has historically viewed women.

When the Prophet (PBH) brought the Revelation of God to humanity, women were living in a degraded state. They were subjected to brutal tribal rituals and were considered to be almost subhuman. For example, infant daughters on the Arabian peninsula were sometimes buried alive because it was considered to be shameful to bear a female child. For the women living in the region where Muhammad (PBH) first revealed His prophecies, Islam was a new lease on life, an opportunity to be equally treasured by humankind.

Islam brought true freedom to women. It offered a broad horizon for the expression of each woman's personality and her way of life. It created a set of ideals and helped women to shape their leadership roles and duties. Women became part and parcel of the community and society as a whole, rather than being pariahs and outcasts. The Qur'an and *Sunnah* are rich with examples of women who led meaningful lives of dignity and worth and made valuable contributions to their societies.

The first Islamic state in which the Prophet (PBH) was chosen to rule was Medina. In A.D. 622, a constitution called the *sahifa* was drawn up, detailing the governing principles for an Islamic state. The *sahifa* stipulated the rights and duties of all its citizens, both men and women. Women were granted full participation in prayers, education, and social and political aspects of the state. In addition, women received full economic independence.

This was a time not only of social and economic growth but also of spiritual growth for women, who became important teachers of Islamic law and tradition. Until 800 years ago, certain learned women were allowed to preach at the pulpit of the Omayad Mosque in Damascus. The "Sahih El Bukhari" is an authentic text containing the traditions of the Prophet Muhammad (PBH). According to Samar Al-Asha, a woman author who has collected the references in El Bukhari that had been authenticated by women, dozens of women were authorities in the teaching of *Hadith* (oral traditions attributed to the Prophet [PBH]). One example is Sayida Aisha, the wife of the Prophet (PBH) and one of the sources of knowledge of Islamic *Hadith* and traditions. Among the many other narrators of *Hadith* were Asma Bint Abu Baker, Fatima Bint El Minzer, Joueriya Bint El Harith, Hafza Bint Omar, and Zainab Bint Gahsh.[1]

As Islam spread through the world, the knowledge it contained brought light to the different cultures it touched. In the fourteenth century, Muslims participated in the new renaissance of science and literature of their time, contributing knowledge and advances from which the modern world is still benefiting. However, the process was reciprocal, and the values of surrounding cultures exercised an influence on Islam. Islam was subjected to the integration of many cultural practices that existed prior to the religion. These values were not intrinsic to the teachings of the Prophet (PBH) but inclined more toward the particular tribal culture of each given society. Some of them involved oppression of women.

It is important to distinguish between authentic Islam and cultural accretions, and to examine the built-in mechanism within the Islamic faith for adapting to cultural surroundings. *Shariya* and the *Akida* (the foundation of faith) cannot be changed. However, the religion makes provisions for a process called *ijtihad*, which is designed to allow the tenets and practices of Islam to adapt to the specific needs of a given culture and generation. *Ijtihad* is not a free-for-all in which people can cut, snip, and mold the religion to suit the changing whims of cultural bias. Rather, the process is based on specific criteria and ultimately on an overarching foundation called *Wa La Darrar Wa La Derrar*, the obligation to serve the cause of justice without discrimination based on wealth, power, gender, race, or color. It is very clear, then, that cultural adaptation does *not* validate the oppression of any group of human beings, including women.

ISLAM AND WOMEN— A CLOSER LOOK AT THE TEXTS

Now let's look at some specific quotations from the Holy Qur'an dealing with women.

O Mankind, reverence your guardian Lord Who created you from a single soul and out of it created its mate and from them twain scattered like seeds countless men and women. He created many pairs. Fear Allah through whom ye demand your mutual rights, and be heedful of the wombs that bore you, for Allah ever watches over you. (Chapter 4, *El Nissaa*—Women, verse 1)

O Mankind we have created you from male and female and we have made you into nations and tribes that you may know each other. Indeed the best of you is the most pious of you. It is Allah who is the Knower. (Chapter 49, *El Hujurat*—The Compartments, verse 12)

These verses define the foundation of the relationship between men and women and humanity as a whole. They state clearly that both men and women are creations of God. Both have rights. Men must respect women, whose wombs bore them. And what is the purpose of creation? Both men and women were created to engage in relationships of "knowledge" and "piety." There is no implication that one group should dominate the other or that one group possesses special "knowledge" about the other. On the contrary, it is God who is the Knower. And the superior individual is the one who is the most pious, not the one who is male.

This sentiment is echoed in the following verse:

Whoever works righteousness, man or woman, and has faith, verily to him/her will we give a life that is good and pure, and we will bestow their reward according to the best of their actions. (Chapter 16, *El Nahl*—the Bee, verse 97)

Again, the measuring rod of worth is not gender but virtue. Rewards will be meted out to "whoever works righteousness—man or woman," who has faith and lives a good, pure life.

Now let's introduce another dimension to the picture that the Qur'an paints of men and women. God created the two sexes not only to serve Him but also to find love with each other. This is a little known and often forgotten teaching of Islam:

It is your creator who created you from a single soul and made his mate
of like nature in order that he might dwell with her in love. (Chapter 7,
Al Arraf—The Heights, verse 189)

The Prophet Muhammad Himself (PBH) regarded women with the
utmost respect. For example, one of His companions, a man named
Anas, quoted Him as saying "women are the sisters of men."

Having cited important verses demonstrating the high regard in
which Islam holds women, I will turn to some of the most commonly
misunderstood concepts. For example, it is said that women should remain in their homes. This concept has been grotesquely misapplied and
abused by the Taliban, who imprisoned women in their houses and did
not allow them to go out. They were distorting the meaning of the following verse in the Qur'an:

O consorts of Prophet ye are not like any of the other women. . . . Stay
quietly in your houses and make not a dazzling display, like that of the
former times of ignorance, and establish regular prayer and give *zakat*
[charity] and obey Allah and His messenger. Allah only wishes to remove all abomination from you, ye Members of the family [of the
Prophet (PBH)] and make you pure and spotless. (Chapter 33, *El
Ahza*—The Confederates, Verses 32–33)

To begin with, the instruction to remain in the house was addressed
specifically to the wives of the Prophet (PBH). It is clear that the family of the Prophet (PBH) was being asked to observe a higher standard
of piety than other people. The opening words of the passage above
spell this out, distinguishing between the Prophet's (PBH) wives and
other women.

A second point is that they were not given a blanket restriction
against going out. On the contrary, they were only abjured not to
make a "dazzling display" of themselves—in other words, not to be
ostentatious or flirtatious. But they had the right to go out for necessary reasons and obligations. It is clear that they were also accorded

a special social position as consorts of the Prophet (PBH)—they were to give charity, engage in prayer, and serve as fountains of knowledge for others. It has been documented in many books of tradition that Islamic women were encouraged to pray, learn, and even teach in the mosques. The Prophet (PBH) specifically said, "Do not prevent the women from going to the mosques and they are to go out with modesty."

Women's role in society is not merely defined in negative terms—that is, that they are *not* to be imprisoned, *nor* to be oppressed—women are considered to be active participants in the formation of policy. The original Arabic words read, "Wa umrahum shura binahum" (Take your matters by consultation). These words mean that according to divine instruction, a Muslim ruler must conduct the affairs of the society by consulting with its members—including women.

WOMEN AND ISLAM—
A CLOSER LOOK AT HISTORY AND PRACTICE

As mentioned, women were authentic transmitters of oral traditions, called *Hadith*. Transmitters of *Hadith* were El Sahih Bukhari, Muslim, and Tirmithi. These scholars made painstaking efforts to authenticate every saying of the prophet. Every *Hadith* required careful investigation and corroboration. Many scholars believe that women were considered to be authentic and wholly trustworthy sources of tradition, as fully respected as men. Another scholar, Al Showkani, said, "The scholars have never stated that any fact [offered by a woman] was rejected [merely] because she was a woman."

Women were in large measure responsible for the rapid dissemination of Islamic teachings, according to Islamic chronicler Al Waqadi, who was born in A.D. 747 and whose work was compiled by his student Ibn Sad in his book *Kitab-al tabaqat al kubra* (Book of Classes). This renowned work contained the biography of 600 women named as companions or disciples of the Prophet (PBH). One hundred and fifty of these women were responsible for the recounting of over a thousand traditions in all aspects of life and not only those pertinent to women's issues.

It is clear that these statements reflect not only the faith and loyalty of the women who aligned themselves with the cause of the Prophet (PBH) but also their level of education and spiritual proficiency. One cannot transmit a teaching one has not learned. The Prophet (PBH) clearly trusted women to be the recipients as well as the teachers of spiritual truths.

The following is a partial list of historical circumstances in which women played an important role:[2]

- Women played an active role in the society and the mosques.
- One of the Prophet's (PBH) wives, Zeinab Bint Gahsh (*umm el moumanin,* the mother of all believers), worked by her hand and gave her own charity.
- A woman named Umm Salam negotiated and advised the Prophet (PBH) regarding *sulh el hadibya* (the first Islamic treaty).
- Women sat in mosques. As the ruler Ummar was addressing a congregation in a mosque, he attempted to simplify the portion of dowry to a measurement of wheat. A woman raised her voice to challenge his interpretation, reminding him that the correct measurement was of gold. He admitted that the woman was right and he was wrong.
- One of the first recorded members of a security force was actually a woman. Her name was Samara. She enjoined what was righteous and she forbade what was incorrect. She wielded authority over both men and women.
- *Hijab* (the head scarf), a protection or a veil, has been an instrument of oppression in many societies. The obligation of women is to cover only the head and chest *(khimar).* When the Prophet (PBH) was asked about the obligation of women to be covered, he

responded by showing his face and hands. *Hijab* has been an instrument of protection and modesty for women.

- There are many examples of women who were independently employed and empowered to make financial decisions. For example, Zeinab, daughter-in-law of Masood, worked by her hand and spent her earnings on her husband and her stepchildren. Umm Atia shared in her husband's work. She was even allowed in the military and is recorded as having participated in six wars.

- Women had more choices in marriage than is believed. For example, Hafsa, the daughter of Omar, a companion of the Prophet (PBH), asked Ali bin Abdallah bin Omar for his hand in marriage. In fact, it is specifically forbidden by Islamic law to force women into marriages against their will. Women have the right to choose their husbands.

- A woman has the right to leave her husband. The word in Arabic for when a woman asks for divorce is *khulu*. An example of a woman who did this is Habiba Bint Sahl Ibn Thalaba, who married a wife-beater named Thabit Ibn Quis. She consulted the Prophet (PBH), who told the husband to divorce her.

- A woman named Zeinab Bint Mahgar stood up to disagree with Abu Baker El Siddique, the first ruler of Muslims in Medina after the death of the Prophet (PBH).

- A woman named Ummaya Bint Quis Al Ghafary went to the Prophet (PBH) together with some other women. They requested permission to go out to *khaybar* (the battlefield) to assist the Muslim cause and also treat wounded men. The Prophet (PBH) answered, "Go with the blessings of Allah."

- Someone asked the Prophet, "Who is worthy of my care first?" The Prophet said, "Your mother." He asked again, "Who is worthy of my care first?" The Prophet said, "Your mother." He asked again, "Who is worthy of my care first?" The Prophet said, "Your mother." He asked again, "Who is worthy of my care first?" The Prophet said, "Your father."

CONCLUSIONS

I would like to conclude with the words of Hind Bint Uqba Ibn Rabia, a woman who pledged her allegiance to the Prophet (PBH) in the form of a poem. I dedicate this poem to the women of Afghanistan and to women around the world who are living in affliction:

> Destiny is against us, we are unable to resist.
> It was an outburst of battle after battle.
> For every man needed to avenge a friend.
> What pain my eyes have seen at the death of my men.
> Tomorrow, how many men and women will join the women in battle;
> How many were left to die in the pit
> The dawn of that fierce cry! All courageous men in those arid years
> When the sky withheld its rain
> I was afraid by what came before my eyes, and now it is realized.
> I was frightened by what came before my eyes, and today I am helpless.
> Tomorrow, men and women will say sorrowfully, "O pity for the
>   mother of a son."
>
> —translated by Sanaa Nadim

This poem resonates even today, centuries after it was written. At the dawn of this millennium, women are still suffering in many parts of the world. There is a lack of knowledge and education about the true meaning of a woman's existence and her role in society. The reality is that the struggle of women is universal. Only the degree and form of injustice vary. In the Western world, domestic violence against women is on the rise. Despite strides in the direction of equal employment opportunities, women are still struggling to become chief executive officers in the corporate setting. In China and Russia, women are still being sold in slave markets, and in some parts of Africa, little girls are still being subjected to barbaric rituals of circumcision.

Islam has a great deal to enlighten the modern world about men, women, and their peaceful and respectful coexistence. It is clear that the Taliban and others who seek to confine and suppress the voices of women have not studied the Qur'an properly, nor are they familiar with Islamic history. It is time for the authentic voice of Islam to be heard by both Muslims and non-Muslims alike. It is time to reach into the true past of Islam, beyond the boundaries of man-made culture and misinterpretation, and bring back the teachings that can transform our lives today. I am proud to be what God has created—a woman. I am blessed by being not only the cradle of life, the source of the very perpetuation of human existence, but also a partner in the continuous progress of civilization and the evolution of human morality and spirituality.

I believe that the women of Afghanistan must continue to struggle to find their place in the world according to their own moral convictions. Although the West can play an important role in the reconstruction of Afghanistan, I do not believe that this means the imposition of alien values on Afghan women. The ultimate goal of Western intervention should not be an attempt to alter the inherent value system of Afghan women. Afghan women must find their path according to their own spiritual and intellectual vision. They must come to terms with their choices and struggle for their coexistence under the new government. They must work toward their own peace accord.

NOTES

1. Samar Al-Asha, *Al Tayseer Fi Hafz Al Assaneed/Assanid Sahih El Bukhari* (Authoritative References of *Hadith* by Women) (Syria: 1998).
2. More information on the role of women can be found in Abdul Alhalim Mohammed Abu Shaqa, *Tahrir Al Amaraa Fi Asr Al Rassala* (Cairo, Egypt: 1995).

THE *ZAN* OF AFGHANISTAN

A 35-Year Perspective on Women in Afghanistan

Arline Lederman

THE DRAMA OF THE *CHADARI*,[1] the cruelty of the Taliban, and limited knowledge of Afghan history have led us to oversimplify both the difficult struggles and enormous strengths of the *zan* (the word means "women" in Farsi) of Afghanistan. Reality is richer and more complex than our headlines reveal.

The mountains of Afghanistan over eons compressed the earth into precious jewels and metals. The land of Afghanistan over centuries condensed numerous peoples and their cultures into a rich and varied nation. The women of Afghanistan are as varied, resilient, and multifaceted as the hidden jewels and many civilizations their land has hosted.

We have come to know of the terrible suffering the women of Afghanistan endured under the Taliban. The oppressors themselves were victims of religious fanaticism, ignorance, poverty, and vestiges of social values created over previous centuries. They visited their cruelty upon the far more evolved Afghan society through domination of the women.

But Afghan women have not always been the downtrodden, oppressed figures who have emerged in recent years, trembling behind blackened windows and stuffed under *chadaris*. It is also important for us to recognize that in 1977 women comprised over 15 percent of Afghanistan's highest legislative body and that by the early 1990s, 70 percent of schoolteachers, 50 percent of government workers, and 40 percent of doctors in Kabul were women.[2] In addition, women throughout the Afghan society were social and economic agents, valued helpmates, and revered leaders. Many Afghan women had rich and varied lives.

I first moved to Afghanistan in 1965 to aid in developing modern educational and cultural institutions. Most outsiders who encountered Afghanistan in that era developed a deep love for the beauty of the country and the warmth and dignity of the Afghan people. My family succumbed immediately, and that love has been with us ever since. Along with teaching at Kabul University and volunteering at a girls' high school, I became a student of the crafts of the country, which I call the Afghan traditional arts. Most of the practitioners of the crafts were women who embroidered, wove, and created great beauty. My husband became a colleague of the academic leaders at the university, where women also held important positions. When all that ended with the Soviet invasion in 1979, we both became advocates for Afghan freedom and helplessly watched while the women were disenfranchised.

As a researcher in the arts before the Soviet invasion, I traveled through Afghanistan and had the privilege of getting to know Afghan women of all regions and levels of society. Later I met many Afghan women in exile. I have never failed to be impressed by their strength of character and their graciousness.

WOMEN IN THE AFGHANISTAN I KNEW

Let me share with you some memories of women I came to know during my stay in Afghanistan. The legal equality of women in Afghanistan had first been established under King Amanollah Shah in the early 1920s. The reaction against many of his attempts at modernization included a rejection of his policy toward women and led to his exile in 1928. Afghan leadership under King Mohammad Zahir Shah, who reigned from 1933 to 1973, made further public attempts to create equal rights for women. In the view of that regime, women and men were equal. Of course, this does not mean that opportunities for women were completely equal throughout society or that women were not victimized in personal or social situations. A lag existed between official policy and its enactment on a day-to-day level throughout society. This situation was not exclusive to Afghanistan. In all societies, the practical implementation of visionary new laws takes time, and there is a great deal of variation in the way new laws promoting equality for the sexes have been put into practice. In the West, opportunity frequently depends on numerous factors beyond ability, including economic and educational as well as gender factors.

In 1964, King Mohammad Zahir Shah called a *loya jirga* (representative council of leaders) for the promulgation of a new constitution. The result of that *jirga* was a constitution that should still be what Louis Dupree, a historian of Afghanistan, called "a model for all of the Muslim world." According to Dupree, debate at that constitutional convention included serious discussion regarding the role of women and the extent to which equality should be explicitly spelled out by the new constitution. Some women delegates wanted to be certain that women would be clearly and explicitly granted rights, but "finally a woman member withdrew her proposal for the special mention after a most meaningful discussion where the constitutional committee assured her that the word 'Afghan' embraced both sexes." Dupree goes on to state, "The emphasis on the legal equality of women is one of the more important aspects of the 1964 Constitution."[3]

That decision positively affected Afghan society. It showed in women's dress. In the summer of 1965, the Afghan women I met in Kabul dressed in chic French fashions at private parties, in pleated blue *chadaris* in the public bazaar, and in embroidered headscarves—most often bright red, with gold trim—on the paths of the Silk Road as they walked in the open with their camels and sheep. Even the most visible level of Islamicized or acculturated attire, that of veiling or modesty in dress, was greatly varied and defined primarily by socioeconomic microsocieties. Afghan women had choices in how they veiled and how they dressed, at least in the larger sense if not in the particular.

The U.S. State Department Briefing Book on Afghanistan for newly assigned employees in 1965 showed photos of the women of the Afghan royal family. The book featured well-coiffed women wearing raincoats and stylish sunglasses, Hermès headscarves, and gloves. They could have passed for Jackie Kennedy's friends on an autumn day in Boston, but they were attending a formal function in Kabul. The photo was designed to inform American women moving to Kabul about the local public dress mores. In contrast, at that time our own society was still constrained. The same book advised American women to bring white gloves, hats, stockings, and girdles to be appropriately dressed for the diplomatic corps occasions. For an avant-garde New York intellectual, the American mores seemed more exotic and restrictive than the Afghan ones.

Along with the varieties of dress were many choices in personal identities for women in Afghanistan in the 1960s and 1970s. Some were educated in Europe, others in Turkey, and in the United States on scholarships. Some women, like the men, were educated only by hard work on the farm or as herders and pastoral nomads. Some women were world-class master craftswomen who wove splendid Turkoman carpets of great economic value to family and to the country. Each woman carried with her another framework for what it meant to be a woman, and those frameworks resulted from her unique set of circumstances—family, tribe, geography, and cultural norms.

Female Afghan engineering students studied in coed classes in the University of Kabul in 1965. My husband did not have women undergraduate engineering students at Stevens Institute of Technology in Hoboken, New Jersey, until 1970! In 1965 my husband shared an office with an Afghan woman professor of mathematics, who held a master's degree. That was a full decade before he had women colleagues in the United States.

Let us look at implications of another aspect of pre-Taliban life for Afghan women—the wearing of a *chadari*. Members of the Hazara tribe, because of their minority Shiite religion, relative poverty, and distinctive Mongol looks, were (and still are) subjected to prejudice in Afghanistan. As a group they had limited economic opportunity and worked at difficult jobs, such as the farming of small plots of land and hard day labor. The women in the city of Hazarajat mostly went around with a headscarf, not a *chadari*, which is both impractical for their lives and expensive. When Hazara families moved to Kabul for economic opportunities, the men often went to work outside the home while the women worked in the house. These newly transported families frequently accumulated enough money for the women to sport the sign of middle-class prosperity, the sign that they no longer needed to engage in outdoor labor—the *chadari*.

If you were a foreigner in Kabul and employed a nanny for your children, she was most likely a Hazara grandmother, past child-bearing age. She was unveiled at work. These women saw an opportunity to work in the foreign community and earn salaries well beyond those of most men in the country. Many of the shopkeepers in Kabul were also Hazara and were rapidly accumulating wealth and educational opportunities for their children.

According to some scholars, the heavy tent-like veil worn by women in the Near East and eventually by Muslims started with upper-class Christian women of the Ottoman Empire. For status, safety, and comfort, they were frequently carried about in curtained sedan chairs, which were similar to the sedan chairs of the Hindu aristocracy or European royalty. The chairs enabled riders to avoid the mud of rough roads that would sully their finery. The coverings offered privacy and protection from thieves and from dust. Some Near Eastern historians believe that the complete covering was an imitation of upper-class Christian female style rather than a Muslim religious requirement.

The Qur'an requires modesty in female dress but does not specify that a woman must be covered from head to toe. Certainly it does not require or recommend the seclusion and virtual imprisonment of women that took place under Taliban rule. Indeed, according to the literature, Mohammad himself had four wives with career skills. It is well known that his first wife was a successful entrepreneur. The Taliban and other self-styled contemporary religious conservatives never seem to acknowledge that fact or to distinguish between theology and custom.

Most women in any society will tell you that men typically try to dominate women and that women need to be vigilant and fight to maintain equality of power and control over their own lives. Poverty and war exacerbate the tendency to dominate the vulnerable. Religion is frequently the vehicle used (or abused) to legitimatize domination in all societies. Many social analysts, however, believe that control over economic assets is really the most significant motivation and that religion is just an excuse. Possibly the Mid- and Near Eastern traditions of cloistering and the domination of women came from economic and social turmoil. The Qur'anic laws favoring men in areas such as inheritance and dowries are not to be discounted as ever-tempting motivators, assuring men access to greater wealth. In Afghanistan, women were active in securing rights to protect children, assets, and land.

COMPARING WOMEN'S ROLES IN THE UNITED STATES AND AFGHANISTAN

I am old enough to remember when most women in the United States did not smoke on the street, when they wore gloves for public occasions and put on hats, tailored suits, and high heels before leaving the house. Slacks were acceptable only in the country or for sports. So let us not focus too strongly on dress and the veil as the single significant factor distinguishing Afghan from American women. Part of what I remember about United States history was a push to remove women from the workforce during the post–World War II years to make jobs available for the returning soldiers. I also remember being advised by older friends to not be too ambitious in my academic aspirations, lest I lose out on the opportunity to marry and raise a family. And this occurred in urban, prosperous, and educated East Coast America in the 1950s. I also remember a professor telling me in the 1960s that women did not teach in universities! Many other women and I have disproved that notion over the past thirty years.

Afghan women in the 1960s faced economic and social disparities and ambiguities of class as well as of societal norms. At the same time as Hazara women were buying *chadaris,* a dear Afghan friend, who had earned a higher degree from Columbia University, was wearing a miniskirt and white high-heeled Courrège boots while teaching at the university. I cringed at some of her encounters on the public bus, where she did not hesitate to take on conservative critics. She was the new Afghan woman of the 1960s. I have just learned that her mother was the talented seamstress who made her stylish clothes, including the miniskirts, at home in Kabul.

HISTORY OF WOMEN IN AFGHANISTAN

Afghanistan was isolated from significant foreign intercourse from the eighteenth century to the 1950s. King Habibollah Shah, who reigned from 1901 to 1919, promulgated a series of acts designed to bring about modernization. Habibollah made a public statement against discrimination by marrying women of different ethnicities. Thus he created access to the central government for all regional leaders. Although the notion of marrying off women for political or military purposes is outrageous and demeaning to Westerners, this move played an important role in Afghan history and underscored the powerful position women could hold in Afghan society.

In the early 1920s, King Amanollah emulated Ataturk of Turkey in sending talented young people abroad to attain the highest-quality Western education. He was grooming them to become national leaders. He also insisted on emancipating women as part of his process of creating a more modern country. He had traveled in Europe and knew that educated, free women could contribute significantly to society. King Mohammad Zahir Shah was largely educated in France and, following his father, King Mohammed Nadir Shah, continued to unify and modernize the country after a regressive period of rebellion following Amanollah. He sent women as well as men abroad to be educated and respected their intelligence and contributions to society.

By the 1960s, King Zahir Shah resolved to educate all Afghan youth to international standards, to emancipate women fully, and to gradually enter the community of nations as a full participant in world affairs. Each of these goals had to be approached cautiously since tribal and isolated peoples do not quickly change their ways.

In the 1960s and 1970s, Afghan women were sent all over the world through foreign education programs to earn higher degrees in leading universities. They returned to become professionals in their own country. In fact, Afghanistan had the highest percentage of foreign students who returned to their own country after receiving their foreign training.[4] Professors at the university, doctors at the hospitals and new medical schools, members of the ministries, lawyers and judges in the courts, and entrepreneurs of all sorts emerged during this era. They helped move Afghanistan forward socially and economically. It was a thrilling time.

Afghan women often appeared to perform what I believed was the impossible. They managed to remain gracious homemakers while simultaneously developing their careers. What made that possible, in part, was the support of their warm extended families. In part it was also the Afghan women's tradition of putting family first. And in part it was the availability of inexpensive help as well as the determination to have it all—a sentiment similar to that driving women of the West.

During my Fulbright research year in 1977–78, I had the opportunity to travel over every passable road in Afghanistan and many roads that were nearly impassable. In almost every village of any size, I saw young girls skipping to school in matching black uniforms with their white headscarves flying. They symbolized the rapid evolution of national education in Afghanistan, the accomplishments of Mohammad Zahir Shah, and the gradual strengthening of representative democracy. I hope we will see that sight again soon.

The Soviet invasion of Afghanistan, devastating though it was, brought further positive evolution to the public Afghan woman. Veils in urban areas were almost completely gone, jobs for women were mostly open, and equality was frequently presumed and certainly stated. Schools were expanded throughout the country, and women went to them with great success. The price—loss of freedom for all members of society under the repressive Communist regime that economically abused Afghanistan—was too high. Correctly, Afghans refused to pay that price. But the role of women definitely evolved in a forward direction during those years.

The failure of the West or the United Nations to take an active role in rebuilding the nation after the Soviet defeat in 1992 left a dangerous power vacuum, which was filled by the lowest common denominator. First the rapacious warlords and then the primitive religionists, the Taliban, seized power. Drug money, oil money, political control of territory, and economic control of society were all part of their hidden agenda. In my view, Islamic fundamentalism was just the vehicle by which they—the Pakistani Interservices Intelligence (ISI) with a lust for territory to hold their burgeoning population, Pashtun billionaire drug lords from the Northwest frontier, and possibly double-agent Saudis with desire to control the future of oil resources and religious propagation—gained and maintained power.

There was enough wicked will among the Taliban to take those girls out of school and lock them up at home. There was enough stupidity to take women from their jobs and forbid them to go outside. The repression was a result of deep ignorance and malicious manipulation rather than authentic religious knowledge and commitment. Indeed, throughout history repression of women in the name of religion has been a favorite activity of those who wish to dominate others. Orthodox Catholics and fundamentalist Christians, Orthodox Jews and Orthodox Muslims all have exercised absolute control of women as a tactic at various times in history. This strategy had the advantage of preventing 50 percent of the competition from inheriting land and other assets. Perhaps most important, men with a profound sense of inadequacy due to poverty or ignorance could wield power and thereby gain a sense of self-esteem and control. This approach continues to appeal to many men in societies throughout the world. Mid- and Near Eastern countries do not have a monopoly on this type of male domination.

Osama bin Laden cleverly manipulated the Taliban for political power. They were mostly poor foot soldiers from primitive and impoverished homes. It was easy to work them into a frenzy over what they were taught to believe was religious truth. They were vulnerable and easy to control. The repression of women was an attractive element to this band, but it was almost incidental to the actual purposes for which these soldiers were used. Dominating women was a simple way to organize and embolden young men, but the real goal was land, access to the oil of Uzbekistan, concealment of a billion-dollar drug business, and progress toward a central independent Pashtunistan that could be annexed to Pakistan.

The Pashtunistan issue has long simmered in the region. Pashtuns (also called Pathans) are found on both sides of the Afghan Pakistani border. *Paktunwali,* or the Pashtun code of honor, which emphasizes the purity of women, is a symbol of their culture. Was this cloistering a weird parallel to the chivalric code of the Middle Ages? Was this repression of women a strange twist on the Islamic need to protect family?

Was it a distorted sense of male domination for primal purposes? What-ever its origins, it became the rallying flag of the Taliban control of Afghanistan. It enabled the Taliban leaders to turn a band of primitive, hungry, discontented men into an "army" with a sense of purpose and an organizing principle. This army, now unified around the repression of women, would serve many other useful and far more important ends.

The social and economic cloistering of women and the removal of women from active and creative lives are sure signs of a dysfunctional society. Throughout history, constant vigilance has been required to guard against the degeneration of society into barbarism and primi-tiveness. The world's failure to be vigilant in post-Soviet Afghanistan resulted in intolerable conditions for that country and, in turn, intol-erable conditions for Afghan women. We have an obligation, as citizens of the world, to see that post-Taliban Afghanistan restores dignity to women. All human society will benefit as a result.

Our obligation to ensure the continued march of civilization—eth-ical, fair, just treatment for all human beings, especially women—does not stop with our involvement in Afghan affairs. A failure to speak up regarding female genital mutilation, unequal employment opportuni-ties for men and women, sexual exploitation in the family or the work-place, family health issues, and inequities in educational opportunities—to name just a few areas where women are oppressed—will reverberate throughout our small planet. We cannot regard what happens in one part of the world as being "their" problem. What hap-pens to some women affects all women. What happens to some human beings affects everyone. We learned on September 11 how events in far-away Afghanistan could reach into our own homes.

CONCLUSION: A TAPESTRY OF BEAUTY, A CALL FOR INVOLVEMENT

The women of Afghanistan come from many tribal, social, and eco-nomic groups: Herati women with Persian backgrounds, elegant Persian-based educations, and refined tastes; Turkomen women, who weave exquisitely and are prized as wives, and who also have enormous economic power; Kochi or nomad women, who herd goats and make cheese, whose fathers threaten them with marriage to male villagers if they don't behave—these are but a few groups of Afghan women. There are also Hazara, women whose husbands show off their felt carpet work. I have encountered Aimaq, Arabi, and Uzbeq women, whose husbands take pride in their embroidery and weaving. I have met urban Persian speakers, whose wives teach, write poetry, and work as journalists, and whose daughters attended the university. I have spoken to Pashtun women doctors, who practice in hospitals. I have found for the most part that men cherish their wives and treat them as respected equals. I have found that all the groups want better, safer, and more fulfilling lives for their children, including their daughters.

What we have then is a complex picture of life for women in Afghanistan. We cannot talk about Afghan women as if they are a generic, monolithic being. Class, opportunity, economics, ethnicity, religion, and culture all factor into what women can achieve. This is the reality for women all over the world.

There is no room in the reborn Afghanistan for misinterpretations of religion. Afghanistan must be helped to develop into what it can be and what it was well on its way to becoming before the self-interested Soviet invasion and the cruel and cynical Taliban destruction. We rejoice along with our Afghan friends that world events have opened a window of opportunity to a future for Afghanistan that includes a hopeful life for its beautiful daughters.

NOTES

1. The Afghan term for the head-to-toe pleated covering, usually called the *burqa* (an Arabic word) in the West. Sometimes spelled *chadri*.
2. UNICEF, *The State of the World's Children*, 1989.
3. Louis Dupree, *History of Afghanistan* (Princeton, NJ: Princeton University Press), 1980, p. 578.

4. Information about students returning to Afghanistan following training in the United States is based on the experience of the USAID program to establish an indigenous college of engineering at Kabul University between 1963 and 1973. See "Kabul Afghan-American Program," Final Report AID/nesa–76 (Afghanistan),1963–1973.

EXCERPTS FROM
THE APOSTLE'S DIARY

ELIZABETH GOULD
AND PAUL FITZGERALD

Preface from *The Apostle's Diary: The Journey from Journalist to Quasi-Diplomat to Apostle for Afghanistan,* by Elizabeth Gould and Paul Fitzgerald (to be published)

IN 1977 WE BEGAN WORK together on documentaries of pressing public importance. Big things were happening that year with new approaches to old problems as the Carter administration vowed to eliminate the threat of nuclear war, reopened the gates to Cuba, and reevaluated détente with the Soviet Union. The Strategic Arms Limitation Treaty (SALT) was a major vehicle for these changes, and by 1979 we had come to focus on its impact by interviewing the central figures.

In that summer of 1979 we had no idea that distant, insignificant Afghanistan would soon erupt as a flashpoint between East and West or that events there would rock the world for twenty-two years.

As the first journalists to view life behind Soviet lines in 1981, we went to Afghanistan with questions. Who were these people? Why had the Soviets invaded? Had they realized the consequences of their actions? Was Afghanistan truly another step in a Soviet desire for world conquest, or was it just another bargaining chip in the seemingly endless give-and-take of Cold War politics?

Prior to September 11, with the Soviet Union and the Cold War just a memory, the idea that Afghanistan still had much to do with the health and well-being of the United States was, of course, unthinkable. But now, with our illusion of security shattered and American troops on the ground in a war that Defense Secretary Donald Rumsfeld suggests might last decades, we must begin to think about the unthinkable while we begin to see the world and our place in it with new eyes. But before we can develop or even suggest credible solutions for what may seem intractable problems, we must first look to the beginning and the events that brought us here.

AFGHANISTAN, 1979:
FULCRUM OF A DELICATE BALANCE

The Soviet invasion of Afghanistan and the U.S. response to it rocked the world. Following America's defeat in Vietnam in 1975 and the fall of Iran in 1979, the invasion was officially viewed as a long-awaited thrust by the Soviet Union toward the Persian Gulf and a dangerous threat to American interests.

In early December of 1979, we had just finished a documentary called the *Arms Race and the Economy, A Delicate Balance,* which analyzed the effects of increased defense spending on the U.S. economy. After a decade of good relations and détente with the Soviet Union, our documentary was received by our television audience with great interest. Then on the night of December 27, 1979, the Soviet Union sent an army of 75,000 troops into Kabul, seized the presidential palace, overthrew the Marxist government of Hafizullah Amin, and installed longtime Communist Babrak Karmal as the new Afghan president.

Weeks later, in an attempt to manage the public's furor over the growing insurrection, the government of Afghanistan expelled 1,135 Western journalists, leaving what President Carter had labeled "the greatest threat to peace since the Second World War" cloaked in a veil of darkness.[1]

Based solely on this event, all discussion of arms limitation and détente, all dialogue with the Soviet Union, even the acceptance of the legitimacy of the Soviet Union itself, seemed to cease. But what intrigued us more was how the bipartisan reaction to the invasion moved the United States away from the policies of détente, mutual cooperation, and negotiation for the first time in a generation. Within months we witnessed not only the dismantling of the SALT negotiations but a near-complete suspension of the cautionary approach to nuclear weapons born of the Cuban missile crisis. The publication of an article in *Foreign Policy* in the summer of 1980 really caught our attention.

In an article titled "Victory Is Possible," Colin Gray and Keith Payne laid out an astonishingly new vision of what was to become the Reagan Doctrine. "If American nuclear power is to support U.S. foreign policy objectives," they wrote, "the United States must possess the ability to wage nuclear war rationally."[2]

Since 1945 the United States had struggled with the idea of using its nuclear weapons to fight a war but had come up empty-handed. Nuclear war, it seemed, wasn't rational, and thinking anything else was unthinkable. But here were two thinkers from the Hudson Institute, a conservative think-tank, doing just that and justifying their position with a medieval concept known as the Just War Doctrine of the Roman Catholic Church. "Force can be used in a just cause; with the right intent; with a reasonable chance of success; in order that, if successful, its use offers a better future than would have been the case had it not been employed; to a degree proportional to the goals sought, or to the evil combated; and with the determination to spare noncombatants, when there is a reasonable chance of doing so."[3]

Somehow, the Soviet invasion of Afghanistan had not only upended a slow, peaceful process of dialogue and détente with America's archenemy, it had thrown American thinking back to the Middle Ages and into the realm of holy war to justify what all sides had heretofore considered the absolute madness of nuclear war. As we watched the Washington bureaucracy empty of moderate voices, Afghanistan became the rallying cry for an arms buildup that would effectively disallow public debate about American foreign policy and establish new precedents for clamping down on the media. But after Vietnam and Watergate, how could the media almost en masse take the Afghan story at face value, refusing to question serious omissions in the story that emanated from Washington?

In a *Columbia Journalism Review* article, Jay Peterzell raised a disturbing question:

> years ago significant U.S. assistance to Afghanistan—or lack of it—would have been a major news story. But today many hard questions are not being asked. Among them is whether, in fact, the U.S. wants the Soviets out of Afghanistan, or prefers to make the country Russia's Vietnam. It could be that we are deliberately furnishing just enough aid to keep the insurgency alive but short of victory. In that case the Afghans are paying a heavy price for their role in the global balance of power.

Peterzell goes on to quote Afghan expert Selig Harrison as describing the journalists who "go to Peshawar and sit around the Intercontinental Hotel filing stories based on what religious groups tell them. The kind of work that would lead you to find out what kind of foreign help is going in there, no one is doing to my knowledge."[4]

When the opportunity to enter Afghanistan for an exclusive look presented itself, we jumped at the chance. What followed was a decade-long education in the perception of Cold War reality that brought us inside CBS News, ABC *Nightline,* the PBS system, and to the top floors at UN headquarters. But the most important lesson of our media engagement was an understanding of the dangers of Cold War journalism and its tendency to oversimplify a complex situation.

Seen solely through the prism of superpower confrontation, Afghanistan was a simple story of Soviet aggression. But seen as a nation being crushed by the forces of modernization, global politics, and extremist Islam, Afghanistan became an entirely different story.

AFGHANISTAN: THE REAL STORY

Struggling to find an identity and grow a modern society in the midst of a war, Afghanistan in 1981 was a myriad of cultural clashes—ethnic, religious, and tribal—the most important of which concerned rights of women and how their role would evolve into the next century. It was in conversations with Kabul's mullahs, the religious leaders working with the government, that we first heard their concern for their religion and culture, calling their tolerant brand of religion "progressive Islam." We listened as they explained their acceptance of women's rights and the absolute need for their country to utilize all of its human resources. But inside a culture caught behind the veil of confrontation between the United States and the Soviet Union, they and millions of others remained ignored.

At the time the scenes on Kabul's streets were dramatic for their normalcy but shocking when compared to the destruction of today. Bustling restaurants filled with diners. Workers hurrying to and from their jobs amid scores of laughing children. A Kabul University where students studied books in English at the American Library. Crowded markets where both men and women worked and shopped. A culture, vast and complex, in the process of evolution. An ancient Afghanistan caught between the three worlds of religion, modern politics, and the Western dream. An Afghanistan that was and could have been.

In the absence of any serious efforts to bring about a better understanding of Afghanistan and in the hopes of finding a solution through negotiation, we invited the Harvard Negotiation Project's Roger Fisher to return with us for a closer look. Arriving in Kabul that spring in 1983, we discovered an Afghan government anxious to begin a dialogue with the United States and the Soviets desperate to get out, their army in disarray, wracked by disease, desertion, and drug addiction.

The war had transformed the Afghan countryside into the second largest opium producer in the world, and many of the "fiercely independent freedom fighters," when not warring against each other, were stockpiling weapons and making themselves rich by exporting drugs. At home in the United States, Afghanistan had become an engine for a multitrillion-dollar military boost of the economy. With the stock market climbing, no one, liberal or conservative, was interested in the Soviets going anywhere.

In the following years we watched as the war escalated and effort after effort failed to bring about a peace. We probed for ways to make sense of the reckless inflaming of a volatile region and came to see that diplomacy always seemed subservient to a hidden agenda. But whose agenda would put Stinger missiles and nuclear technology into the hands of fundamentalist warlords, unstable military dictatorships, and drug dealers?

By the end of the 1980s we had become exhausted and decided to seek answers beyond the day-to-day conflict. Afghanistan had been the cradle of an ancient civilization. Rudyard Kipling, the soldiers' poet, had written about its ancient mysticism and its influence on the West. But what did the intelligence community want with the esoteric secrets of mystical holy warriors?

We experienced great sadness watching the endless progression of the war, knowing there was a deeper level of meaning at work but not being able to find it. We had searched for answers to the Afghan riddle for ten years, but there was little left that we could do.

Then in 1992, when many of the classified documents related to the beginnings of the Afghan war became available, we began again. And as we dug into the political decision making behind the Afghan story, we began to find clues that had eluded us the first time. The geopolitics of Afghanistan had been hiding a deeper meaning, and as we explored the newly declassified documents, we found it.

The holy jihad against the Soviet Union had been as much a religious motivation for the conservative, ideological White House as it had been for the mujahideen (Jehadi Islamic fundamentalists). Possessed with a crusader mentality, the men who had fought and inspired the Afghan holy war against godless communism had found much in common with their "fiercely religious" brethren. United in a common goal, they had sought to redefine the world in the Manichean terms of light against dark, us against them, and in succeeding, they had immersed themselves in an ancient struggle.

Today that war assumes a different guise as B52s pound the hidden caves constructed to protect America's fiercely religious former allies, now turned against us as enemies. But in Afghanistan, where holy war has become a way of life, the struggle continues in what can only be described after September 11 as a war of good against evil.

The Afghanistan we knew in 1980 is gone. But as we face yet another chapter in the history of this small but vital piece of earth, we must ask ourselves the question: "How did it happen?" And if we are to now save Afghanistan from further atrocities, and save the Western world from the terror that has grown there over the last twenty-two years, we must answer fairly and honestly to prevent it from happening again.

NOTES

1. *Presidential Documents,* vol.16 (January 14, 1980), p. 40; "Meet the Press" (January 20, 1980), p. 108; "The State of the Union" (January 23, 1980), p. 196.
2. *Foreign Policy,* Number 39 (Summer 1980), p.14.
3. Ibid., p.16.
4. "The New Afghanistan" (March/April 1981), pp.5, 6.

THE KALEIDOSCOPE OF MEMORY

GLORIA STEINEM

A FEW BLOCKS FROM MY OFFICE at *Ms. Magazine,* terrorism created an inferno that ended this country's separation from the world forever. History and memory show that women are always the first to recognize fundamentalisms and their far-reaching dangers, but their warnings fall on deaf ears.

In 1980, I and other women protested the U.S. support for the mujahideen in their religious war against Afghanistan's Soviet-backed government. The "sins" of this Marxist government were that they encouraged women to attend political meetings, reformed law so that women could marry without parental consent, and sent girls to school. American feminists were ignored, and the United States finally gave a staggering $3 billion in support of religious extremists and gender apartheid.

In the 1990s, fundamentalism was on the rise around the world in many religions, and it was women who were sounding the alarm: American feminists against Christian right-wing extremists who bombed abortion clinics; Indian feminists against Hindu nationalism and Sikh extremism; and Indonesian and Filipina feminists against the Islamic extremism that had taken root in their countries.

In 1996, when the Taliban took over Afghanistan by force, women were beaten and stoned to death for teaching girls to read or failing to conceal every inch of their bodies beneath the shroudlike *burqa*. If the pleas of refugee and underground Afghan women had been listened to—or if women listening here had more influence over foreign policy—Americans would not have been caught unaware by the Taliban and the terrorist network they sheltered.

In the wake of September 11, the Feminist Majority Foundation, the leading U.S. women's group supporting the Afghan women's resistance movement, has been pressuring the U.S. State Department to use that movement to distribute humanitarian aid now and to create a democratic coalition in the future. Instead the Bush Administration has focused on a bombing campaign that has killed more civilians than terrorists, and has helped to unify Islamic countries against us.

Here is what we have learned the hard way: Our greatest danger comes from the normalization of violence through hypermasculinity and vengeful male gods. Our greatest safety comes from supporting only true democracy that honors the full humanity of women and men.

THE MISSION OF RAWA

Freedom, Democracy, Human Rights

Weeda Mansoor

WORLDWIDE, WOMEN ARE FIGHTING to achieve the sacred and trumpeted slogan of "women's rights." Whether black or white, whether in the "rich free world" or in Asia's, Africa's, or Latin America's poverty-blighted countries, whether heterosexual or lesbian, the world's women are individually and collectively part of a common struggle for respect; first as human beings, but also as mothers, sisters, wives, friends, and colleagues.

Women's struggles are as varied and encompassing as humankind itself. Some women are endeavoring to decriminalize abortion, some to eradicate the curses of dowry killings, rape, domestic violence, and *sati*.[1] Some work to eliminate pornography and the trafficking of women and girls for sex and domestic slavery, while others labor to bring an end to prenatal sex selection, the sterilization of impoverished women, and the sale of infant girls in the guise of adoption. Many women fight for equal opportunities and pay in the workplace, others for lesbian rights to marry and raise children, and still others for the right to wear the clothing of choice—to name some of the most common battles around the globe.

We at RAWA stand together with all women, wherever they may be. We weep for our sisters in India, murdered in the name of dowry and *sati*. We share the pain of our sisters in African countries, subjected to female genital mutilation in the name of tradition and religious fundamentalism. We can identify with the experiences of Bosnian rape victims and can stand in their shoes as they face their molesters during the United Nations–sponsored International War Crimes Tribunal in The Hague. Courageous women like Bangladeshi feminist writer Taslima Nasrin, the recipient of death threats from Islamic extremists on the grounds that her writings are blasphemous and un-Islamic, are in our hearts and prayers at all times. And certainly we are in favor of equal opportunities and equal treatment for women everywhere. We consider ourselves, in that sense, fellow feminists and fighters for women's rights.

However, with all due respect to the women of other countries and the struggles they endure, we believe that our struggle is quite different from theirs. It goes beyond social and cultural discrimination, domestic violence, criminal or sexual assault, and equality before the law in private or public situations, although our battle encompasses every one of these areas. While we have these areas of commonality with other oppressed women, there are certain basic differences in the struggles of Afghan women. Simply put, on every level, from "official" government-sanctioned laws to "unofficial" or private acts of brutality, Afghan women are without rights and must battle on a minute-by-minute basis for their very existence. Judges themselves engage in the same abuses of women as common citizens do. To make matters worse, this perilous and egregious state of affairs comes with the sanction of the so-called civilized world, which has empowered, and which continues to empower, our oppressors.

Afghanistan is the world's most forgotten tragedy, the Afghan nation the world's most forgotten population, and her women the most strangulated, ill-fated, and deprived segment of Afghan society. This is not a new phenomenon, though it has worsened in recent years. To understand the magnitude and dimension of this problem, it is necessary to step back and understand the history and context of the human rights abuses against women.

Our enormous suffering began with the Soviet coup d'état of 1978 and increased when the Soviets invaded our country a year later. In 1979 residents of Kabul counted the minutes for the return of their loved ones. Instead, they faced lists naming the prisoners massacred by the Khalq and the Parcham, two factions of the People's Democratic Party of Afghanistan (PDPA). The PDPA, a puppet of the Soviet Union, took power on April 27, 1978, after a bloody coup. They killed thousands of intellectuals in their prisons and killed tens of thousands of people during their bloody rule, which lasted until April 28, 1992, when they were replaced by another even more criminal and brutal regime: the fundamentalists. The Soviet aggressors found new ways to kill freedom fighters—they were known to drop them from helicopters. The Soviets also installed millions of land mines, which, according to the United Nations, still cause many deaths daily.

In the first year of their power, the Soviets seized tens of thousands of freedom-loving people and murdered many of them in the killing fields of Pul-e-Charkhi prison on the outskirts of Kabul. When Afghan women asked about their missing husbands, the answer of officials was: "They were reactionary and were killed. You are free now under our democratic regime to marry another man of your choice." Afghan women were apparently free, but many were used as sex slaves by Soviet officials and soldiers. Many Afghan women have painful stories about those years. When the Soviets finally left the country in 1989, Afghans lived in hope that the darkness and savagery of the past ten years might provide lessons for a peaceful future. We truly believed that no nation, nor any nation's women, could possibly suffer more than we had.

The assault on our women was not conducted only by the Soviets. The Soviets attacked all Afghans—men and women—and people of both sexes lost limbs and lives in the war. But the Jehadi Islamic fundamentalist (mujahideen) bands that fought the Soviets targeted women in horrifying ways. These fundamentalists were created, nurtured, and equipped by Pakistan, Saudi Arabia, Iran, and the United States and its allies during the Cold War. These nations had no interest in the welfare and well-being of Afghans. While their desire to drive the Soviets out of Afghanistan coincided with the wishes of most Afghans, once they achieved their own military and political objectives by supporting the fundamentalists, they abandoned Afghanistan to these conscienceless savages, who turned Kabul and other parts of the country into a bloodbath, with crimes against humanity that made those of the Soviets seem like children's games.

Women and children suffered the most at the hands of the mujahideen, who used Islam as an excuse to commit the most barbaric atrocities. It may surprise Westerners that these fundamentalists form the backbone of the Northern Alliance, which the West has chosen once again to support since September 11. The Northern Alliance, together with the West, has portrayed Masood—its leader, who was assassinated in late 2001—as a "saint." There seems to be a selective amnesia at work here, something that is erasing memory of the terror imposed by the Rabbani-Masood command after the fall of the pro-Soviet puppet regime on April 28, 1992.[2]

A few examples of the brutality perpetrated by the mujahideen should suffice. Recalling the experience, Amnesty International is quoted as reporting:

> armed groups beat, raped and murdered women in their homes. Young women were kidnapped as wives for commanders or sold into prostitution. Some committed suicide to avoid this fate, like one young woman who threw herself off a balcony in her house when soldiers came to kidnap her. In March 1994, a fifteen-year-old girl was repeatedly raped after soldiers killed her father for allowing her to go to school. Many people were victimized for belonging to a certain religious or ethnic group.[3]

Overall, the misogynistic regulations of Rabbani-Masood, Abdurab Rasool Sayyaf, Gulbuddin Hekmatyar, Karim Khalili, and other Jehadi murderers remained in place until their brethren-in-creed, the Taliban, came to power in 1996. As Robert Fisk recounts,

> . . . it remains a fact that from 1992 to 1996, the Northern Alliance was a symbol of massacre, systematic rape and pillage. Which is why we—and I include the U.S. State Department—welcomed the Taliban when they arrived in Kabul. The Northern Alliance left the city in 1996 with 50,000 dead behind it. Now its members are our foot soldiers. Better than Mr. bin Laden, to be sure. But what—in God's name—are they going to do in our name?[4]

After the failure of the Jehadis to fulfill the vicious plans of their masters, another force was unleashed in the battleground of Afghanistan.

> In 1995, the Taliban appeared. They were well-armed and well-organized, and overtook Hekmatyar's forces. Hekmatyar told the *New York Times* that Pakistan's military intelligence wing had likely switched its backing to the Taliban, and *Time* reported in 1996 that captured Pakistani soldiers fighting alongside the Taliban said they had been trained and funded by Pakistan's Interservices Intelligence Directorate (ISI). In 1995, the U.S. finally stopped funding the Mujahideen, but Benazir Bhutto, Prime Minister of Pakistan in 1996, said in a BBC interview that the Taliban training schools in Pakistan had been paid for by the United States and Britain.[5]

The Taliban's human rights abuses, corruption, and deadly and draconian restrictions have been widely documented. While these were directed primarily against women, we will also cite examples of human rights abuses against men, so as to present a balanced picture of the unspeakably brutal regime the United States, Britain, and Pakistan put into power. These restrictions, atrocities, and their results include:

- Women who appeared in public without the *burqa* were physically punished.
- Girls were not allowed to attend school. If a clandestine school was discovered—and many such home-based schools were organized and run by women who had previously been teachers—all involved were physically punished. Although the Taliban eventually allowed a very small number of home-based schools for girls to open in Kabul, only girls under the age of twelve were allowed to attend, and the chief purpose was to teach reading skills so that they could study the Qur'an.
- Women were forbidden to visit a doctor without a close male relative in attendance. Thousands of women were punished when the Taliban caught them at clinics or hospitals. A woman who failed to dress properly or bring a male relative when she visited a doctor could be turned away, even in an emergency. Women died of treatable medical conditions because male doctors were forbidden to treat female patients, and all but a handful of female doctors were barred from practicing medicine.
- Women were forbidden to leave the house without a close male relative and were prohibited from being employed. Barred from any type of employment, thousands of women were, and still are as of May, 2002, forced to beg or enter the flesh business in order to feed their children.
- High-heeled shoes, shoes that made noise, and sandals without socks were prohibited. Women caught wearing stylish clothes or cosmetics—even under the *burqa*—were beaten to the verge of unconsciousness by the Taliban's religious police.
- Public toilets and baths were closed to women.
- Rape and forced marriages proceeded unabated. During the Taliban period and to a lesser extent today, suicide to avoid rape was a common trend among Afghan women and young girls. Although the Taliban's battle cry was the restoration of law and order

after the anarchy of the Jehadis—particularly the gang rapes and murders—the conduct of the Taliban has been equally reprehensible. Gang rape and murder were an everyday occurrence and remain so even after their overthrow.

- Taliban leaders—even those of advanced years—had a penchant for marrying as many as four times. The victims forced into sex slavery were usually young girls, sometimes married to men old enough to be their grandfathers. Polygamy gained momentum, leading to new crimes against women. Often families married off a daughter or sister against her will.

- The Jehadi fundamentalists and the Taliban commonly abducted women and young girls for sex. Abduction remains an alarmingly widespread phenomenon even today.

- Girls were not the only ones to suffer sexual abuse. Both the Taliban and the Northern Alliance sent young boys to the front, where soldiers raped them.

- The Taliban required windows of all homes to be painted black to make it impossible for outsiders to glimpse the women within the house.

- Amputation, stoning, and execution were favorite punishments of the Taliban. Hundreds of women received lashes on their backs for even minor infringements or were stoned to death for alleged adultery. No fair trial or due process was required to convict a woman of such a crime, and no appeal was possible.

- Men were also severely punished if they violated the dress code or prescribed set of regulations. Men without beards, or those whose beards were not of appropriate length, were punished and imprisoned by the Taliban until their beards reached the proper dimensions.

- Shopkeepers were beaten and imprisoned if they were caught trading during prayer time.

- Robbery was punished either by amputation or by death.

- Homosexuality was officially deemed a capital offense and punished by torture, then death.

These obscenities are but the tip of a giant iceberg because the offenses against human rights are carried out not just as "punishment" for infractions of official edicts. Like the Jehadi fighters, the Taliban engaged in a gratuitous set of atrocities against non-Pashtuns and even against their own Pashtun people.

But Afghans were victimized not only by the Taliban; rival fundamentalist groups within the Northern Alliance committed the same brutalities. For example, in the name of religion, barbaric massacres were carried out by Rasool Sayyaf's band and by the pro-Iranian regime Hezb-e-Wahdat (Unity Party) of Karim Khalili. These fighters, now in the Northern Alliance, rose to new heights of brutality and devised a novel series of lethal techniques—crushing people with moving tanks, for example, or hammering eight-inch nails into people's heads. They used the full force of their dark creativity to devise methods of torture, such as setting victims alight in containers, soaking them in burning oil, pumping air into their orifices (mouth or anus) until the body burst, or dragging bodies along rugged paths until the victims died of pain and injury.

Perhaps the most popular technique became known as the "Dance of the Deadbody." The prisoner's throat was slit, but death was prevented by stopping the flow of blood. The victim was then subjected to the successive amputation of hands, feet, and other body parts, then left to writhe in pain until death.

During the last three years, the true and full face of these fanatics was revealed to the Afghan people, but the West remained oblivious and indifferent to the atrocities taking place. They appeared to have no impact on the well-being of Americans, and therefore were not worthy of attention. We cannot stress often enough that it was the United States and its allies who nurtured the most infamous

Afghan fundamentalist groups, including the Taliban, who hosted and harbored Osama bin Laden. There was scant concern for the democratic-minded forces in Afghanistan and the fate of her people when the U.S-supported fundamentalists were placed in power. Vanquishing the former Soviet Union took precedence. Only when the bloodshed reached American soil did Americans wake up, roar, and strike. Let no American life be sacrificed on the altar of American foreign policy! RAWA remains critical of U.S. foreign policy, pointing out that President Bush's support for the Northern Alliance—the newest incarnation of the Jehadi fighters—once again makes a mockery of democracy, women's rights, and human rights values.

Having given the Western reader a glimpse into the enormity of the horror that the Jehadi fighters and the Taliban have inflicted on the Afghan population, with the full support and complicity of the Western world and especially the United States, we will now look at the role RAWA has played in the lives of Afghan women during the years when these atrocities were taking place.

THE HISTORY AND ROLE OF RAWA

The Revolutionary Association of the Women of Afghanistan (RAWA)[6] is an organization founded in 1977 as an independent political/social organization of Afghan women fighting for human rights and social justice in Afghanistan. The founders were a group of female intellectuals under the sagacious leadership of Meena (she did not use a last name), who was assassinated in 1987 by Afghan agents of the Soviet KGB. Her assassins, who carried out their deed in Quetta, Pakistan, were colluding with a fundamentalist band of Afghans under the leadership of Gulbuddin Hekmatyar.

RAWA's original objective was to involve an increasing number of Afghan women in social and political activities aimed at acquiring basic human rights for women and contributing to the struggle for the establishment of a government based on democratic and secular values. Despite the suffocating political atmosphere in Afghanistan, RAWA soon became involved in widespread activities in various sociopolitical arenas, including education, health, income-generating activities for women, and political agitation.

Before the Moscow-directed coup d'état of April 1978, RAWA's activities were confined to agitation for women's rights and democracy. But after the coup and particularly after the Soviet occupation of Afghanistan in December 1979, RAWA became directly involved in the war of resistance. In contrast to the majority of Islamic fundamentalist "freedom fighters" of the anti-Soviet war, RAWA advocated democracy and secularism right from the outset. Despite the horrors and political oppression, RAWA's appeal and influence grew during the years of Soviet occupation, and a growing number of RAWA activists were sent to work among refugee women in Pakistan. RAWA addressed the immediate needs of refugee women and children by establishing schools with hostels for boys and girls and a hospital with mobile teams for refugee women and children in Quetta. In addition, RAWA conducted courses in nursing, literacy, and vocational training for women.

Demonstrations against the oppression of the Soviet invaders and later of the Jehadi fundamentalists, and unwavering commitment to exposing their heinous crimes, have been hallmarks of RAWA's political activities. As a result, RAWA was marked for annihilation by the Soviets and their henchmen, while the fundamentalists vented their wrath on our organization for our pro-democratic, pro-secularist, and antifundamentalist stance. Our uncompromising attitude against these two enemies of our people has cost us dearly—witness the martyrdom of our founding leader and of a large number of our key activists—but we have unswervingly stood, and continue to stand, by our principles.

To propagate our views, aims, and objectives and to give Afghan women a voice as well as social and political awareness regarding their rights and the potential for greater freedom, RAWA launched a bilingual magazine in 1981. *Payam-e-Zan* (Woman's Message) is published in Persian and Pashto[7] on an ongoing basis. English and Urdu issues are available as well. When we started our work, we did not imagine the form it would take in the future and the savagery of our own people against us. We started out by believing that we were fighting foreign invaders; sadly, over the years, we have come to realize that the most insidious enemies come from within the ranks of the Afghan population.

Strikingly, it was Meena—the slain leader of RAWA—who clearly and prophetically foretold the course of events as early as 1982. In an interview with a Belgian TV program during the Soviet invasion, she said, "There are some elements in the country that, due to political interests, seek to create cracks in this national movement. These Afghan fanatics are now present in Peshawar and are willing to have a Khomeni-type of regime for this country."[8]

Like other members of RAWA, Meena had received death threats but no protection from Pakistani police. Her fate is a chilling reminder of what we all risk by doing the work we do. We still face death threats on an almost daily basis. To avoid persecution, the organization has no office, and members are obliged to change residences on a frequent basis. Verbal abuse by different fundamentalist parties as well as by some intellectuals and writers in the service of the fundamentalists is commonplace. They have called us "a bunch of prostitutes," for example, and have threatened us with torture, stoning, and murder for our alleged sexual promiscuity. Those who persecute us have created a series of counterfeit RAWA websites containing pornographic images and text.

We have been labeled anti-Islamic, Maoists, loose women, and infidels. Our organization tries to ignore these slurs on our values and character because we recognize that the sources of abuse are morally bankrupt and pathologically hostile. They grab at anything they think will be effective in marshalling their new Western supporters against us. We are grateful that clear-thinking, informed Western women see through their ruses and acknowledge our true nature and values. For example, Eve Ensler, the noted American novelist, playwright, and activist, commented: "There are a lot of people who say all kinds of false things about RAWA—that they are Maoists, they are Communists. They are very militant, they are very pure. They are very radical. And I'm very drawn to that. People call them uncompromising, and they are right. But bravo! I feel a kindred spirit."[9]

We need to be uncompromising in our work and undaunted by misunderstandings or threats against us. Undeterred by accusations, RAWA continues its work—establishing schools and orphanages in Pakistan's refugee camps; providing mobile health services for women and girls unable to receive care from Afghan physicians; finding ways for Afghan widows to feed their children.

We have been targeted by the Pakistani intelligence, who seek to discredit us and render us incapable of carrying out our mission. Some misguided people have even suggested that we are linked with the Pakistani police! Journalist Aditya Sinha's experience with the Pakistan Interior Ministry indicates that rather than being associated with the Pakistani intelligence, we are targeted and persecuted by them:

the Government of Pakistan directed me to leave. "Immediately," said the Interior Ministry's order, a copy of which was handed to me by the Peshawar Special Branch. Another plain-clothed man arrived on a motorcycle and asked me about my meeting with the secretive Afghan women's group, RAWA. "Who was it you met?" I had to give her name, feeling terrible about what would be in store for her. "Where [did you meet her]?" Fortunately, she had come to my room. "What's her telephone number?"[10]

Because we are considered an illegal organization, we must conduct our operations in secret. Given the clandestine nature of our operation, it is essential for us to clarify our mission and philosophy and our vision for Afghan society and government.

We are inspired by the teachings and blood of our martyred founding leader, who taught us that our women are like sleeping lions who, when awakened, can play a powerful role in any social change. RAWA admits to a feminist philosophy that is not Western-based, although we are willing to learn from feminists in the West. We seek full equality for women in all areas of life, but we regard men as neither the enemy of women nor as the cause of every ill that befalls women or that afflicts the planet. We condemn only those men who regard women as chattel and who deprive them of essential rights.

We regard men and women as partners in a struggle for freedom, democracy, and a society free of any kind of discrimination. We believe that men and women must work together to achieve the dream of an Afghan government that is based on democratic values and that ensures freedom of thought, religion, and political expression while safeguarding women's rights.

Cognizant that fundamentalists use the name of Islam to justify and legitimize their violent madness, RAWA proposes a separation of religious and political processes in Afghanistan. We believe that only a government with a secular orientation can thwart the nefarious designs of these reactionaries from the Dark Ages.

It will be difficult for future government makers to ignore RAWA, the voice of Afghan women and the only independent political feminist organization in Afghanistan. Indeed, it would be a grave mistake to exclude RAWA as the representative of women from any future government that claims to stand for democracy and human rights. The exclusion of RAWA from the UN-convened Bonn accord is disturbing. In the words of Annie Goeke, a Pennsylvania Green Party member: "This [exclusion] shows how women have been continually marginalized in the peace process. . . . RAWA clearly represents one of the most significant voices of the Afghan society."[11] The *Times* of India expressed a widely felt appreciation of our organization:

> The exemplary courage displayed by the RAWA in undertaking such documentation has no parallel in recent history. . . . Armed with hidden cameras, these women have done more to expose the murderous excesses of the Taliban regime than all the international human rights agencies put together. . . . [T]he Afghans have always been credited with an indomitable spirit, which has enabled them to withstand the rapacity of successive invaders. RAWA is living testimony to this.[12]

RAWA'S STATEMENT TO THE WESTERN WORLD

RAWA is steadfast in its assertion that Afghanistan's stability will remain fragile unless it is based on democratic-minded organizations and individuals, including democracy-loving women's organizations. Now that the Northern Alliance have reentered Kabul and have successfully used Bonn as an opportunity to cut a deal for their own interests, the aspirations of a wounded people are once again in jeopardy.

We place before Western readers our experience and perspective—that the Northern Alliance is not the liberator of Afghanistan. Yes, music has returned to Kabul. Yes, men are shaving, cinemas are reopening, and women can be seen on television. But these are the same terrorists who, within days of rising to power in 1992, dynamited the graves of famous popular Afghan singers like Ahmad Zahar and Ustad Sarahan because of their "anti-Islamic" influence on the people. These are the same people who closed the cinemas, banned women from appearing on television, forced women into *burqas,* called schools "gateways to hell" and the television a "devil box."

Since the Bonn conclave succumbed to pressures from the Northern Alliance, the nightmares of 1992 to 1996 loom even larger in Afghanistan's dark skies. While RAWA has yet to secure a position in Afghanistan's future government, it has taken on the courageous and perilous role of informing the international community that the Taliban's place has been taken by a group of fundamentalists of a similar, if not the same, mind-set. The outside world must open its eyes to the fact that the reemergence of the Northern Alliance as the dominant force in Afghanistan may be a greater threat to the safety of the Afghan people than cruise, cluster, and carpet bombs were. RAWA has spelled out the imperative of UN peacekeeping forces and the need for a fundamentalist-free government. For the international community to look away is an indelible stain on human integrity.

NOTES

1. *Sati* is the traditional Hindu practice of a widow immolating herself on her husband's funeral pyre. *Sati* was banned in India in 1829.
2. Burhanuddin Rabbani is the fundamentalist leader of Jamiat Islam Afghanistan (Islamic Association of Afghanistan). During the Soviet regime, he got support from Pakistan's Interservices Intelligence, the CIA, and Arab countries to fight the Soviets. Months after the collapse of the puppet regime in 1992, he became the so-called president of Afghanistan. His forces committed uncountable crimes in Kabul and other provinces.

   Ahmad Shah Masood was the military leader of Jamiat Islami Afghanistan. But he also had another group, the Shurahi Nezar (Supervisory Council). Just days before September 11, he was killed by two Arab suicide bombers in northern Afghanistan. Although a fundamentalist, he fought against the Taliban. From 1992 to 1996, the joint forces of Rabbani and Masood controlled the government in Kabul. During these years they committed numerous crimes against innocent civilians.
3. Kathleen Richter, "Revolutionary Afghan Women," *Z Magazine*, November 2000. See *zena.secureforum.com/Znet/zmag/zmag.cfm*
4. Robert Fisk, "What Will the Northern Alliance Do in Our Name Now? I Dread to Think," *London Independent*, November 14, 2001.

5. Richter.
6. RAWA is based in Afghanistan and Pakistan.
7. The two languages of Afghanistan are Pashto and Dari. According to the author of this article, the difference between Dari and Persian (Farsi) is like the difference between American English and British English. "Persian" is a more popular word than "Dari." Other authors in this volume would disagree with that last point.[Editor]
8. RAWA has a VHS tape of Meena's appearance on Belgian TV in 1982, but we are unable to identify the specific date and show.
9. Eve Ensler, quoted in "Eve Ensler, 'Afghanistan is Everywhere'," by Janelle Brown, *Salon.com,* November 26, 2001.
10. Aditya Sinha, "Pak intelligence investigate journalist for meeting RAWA," *Hindustan Times,* October 28, 2001.
11. Annie Goeke, quoted in "US Green Party News Release," November 27, 2001. See http://www.rawa.org/green2.htm
12. Editorial, *Times of India,* October 29, 2001.

THE *LOYA JIRGA* (GRAND ASSEMBLY) TRADITION IN AFGHANISTAN

WILL THE FORMATION OF A *LOYA JIRGA* EMPOWER WOMEN AND SOLVE THE CRISIS IN AFGHANISTAN?

SARA AMIRYAR

LOYA JIRGA (Pashto words for "grand" and "council") is a historical institution of Afghanistan. Traditionally, insignificant disputes were resolved among parties by a *jirga,* which is a congregation of the elders or prominent people of the village or community. When it came to the national or significant decision-making level, however, the convening of a *loya jirga* was required. Even today, the elders and notables of the ethnic groups and constituencies assemble at such a meeting to discuss and resolve problems that threaten national security or stability. The *loya jirga* plays the key role in choosing new rulers and the mode of government, in declaring war and endorsing treaties of peace, and in supporting important social and civic legislation.

Thus, the traditional *loya jirga* has been of primary importance in the governing mechanisms of Afghanistan. The earliest such assemblies, which took place in the ancient Aryan period (2000–500 B.C.), provided people with a social and political structure. But it was not until the very early eighteenth century, when Afghanistan was divided between Mughals and Persians, that the *loya jirga* became institutionalized. Rebellions against the corrupt local government from Persia arose among the indigenous Pashtun tribes in and around Kandahar, but their disunity and chronic infighting kept them from achieving independence. When Mirwais Khan Hotak, who governed from 1709 to 1715, took steps to unify the rebels by convening groups of respected elderly men from the area, the liberation of Afghanistan was achieved. These *jirgas* were the roots of the far more complex *loya jirgas* of the future, leading up to the Emergency *Loya Jirga* in Kabul, in June 2002.

In 1747, a *loya jirga* composed of Pashtun chiefs convened in Kandahar following the assassination of Nadir Afshar (1688–1747),[1] the Persian king. After deliberating for nine days, they appointed Ahmad Shah Durrani (1722–1773), founder of the Sadozay tribe, the first emir of Afghanistan. Ahmad Shah, the founder of an independent Afghanistan, incorporated the council of chiefs into his rule. Thus he completed the process of formalizing the *loya jirga* that Mirwais had begun and in so doing established the foundation of modern Afghanistan.

Another *loya jirga* assembled when Dost Mohammed Khan (1793–1863), founder of the Barakzay dynasty, overthrew the Sadozais and became the king of Afghanistan (1839–1842). When the British supported Shah Shojah's efforts to seize the Afghan throne because they feared Dost Mohammed's claims to Peshawar and his growing allegiance with Russia, Dost Mohammed called a *loya jirga* to deliberate on the crisis. The result was a declaration of war against Great Britain and the first Anglo-Afghan war (1839–1842). Eventually, the British troops were massacred, and Dost Mohammed was restored to the throne.

In the early twentieth century, Amir Habibollah Khan (1872–1919) convened a *loya jirga* to gain support and approval for his determination to keep Afghanistan permanently neutral in war.

In 1919 King Amanollah Shah (1892–1960), Amir Habibollah's son, held a *loya jirga* to gain support for his policy of revoking the contracts previous kings of Afghanistan had signed with British India. This action, and Amanollah Shah's declaration of independence from Great Britain, caused the third Anglo-Afghan war. Later, King Amanollah Shah convened numerous *jirgas* to get a feel for the national viewpoint on social and political institutions, constitutional issues, and international matters. The king was a strong believer in resolution by *jirga* and in women's rights, and he was committed to the country's rapid development. He believed that Afghanistan's dependent relationship with Great Britain, which had been characterized by large-scale British subsidies, compromised the integrity of Afghanistan as an independent state. In 1929, as a result of Amanollah Shah's unsuccessful attempts to find an alternative source of revenue and military aid and especially because of his efforts to empower women, the tribes and religious movements that had mobilized against his state-building efforts removed him from power and sent him into exile.[2]

In 1945 King Mohammad Zahir Shah had to respond to a Soviet demand that German nationals living in Afghanistan be turned over to them. Since this matter would affect the future relationship of Afghanistan with the world, the king convened a *loya jirga*. It concluded that the Germans should have safe passage to their own country and Afghanistan should remain nonaligned.

In 1955 the relations between Pakistan and Afghanistan began to deteriorate over the issue of Pashtunistan. The partition of India and Pakistan in 1947 had been a catalyst in the Anglo-Afghan dispute over control of the Pashtun and Baluch tribes in the Northwest Frontier region. Afghan rulers wanted to preserve this territory as a buffer zone, if not as part of Afghanistan itself, because the inhabitants of the area were largely Pashtun. When the British left India, Afghanistan hoped the Pashtuns of the Northwest Frontier would have a choice between being independent or joining Afghanistan, but Britain insisted that the Pashtuns join either India or Pakistan. They chose Pakistan because of Islam, their common religion. In 1955 an emergency *loya jirga* met to recommend that Afghanistan should be readied for a war with Pakistan. This assembly, unlike earlier ones, was directed toward national security rather than domestic politics.

In 1963, during the reign of Mohammad Zahir Shah, the *loya jirga* played an important role in establishing the 1964 constitution of Afghanistan. This *loya jirga* consisted of tribal representatives; ethnic leaders; members of both houses of parliament, of the cabinet, and of the judiciary; representatives from civic society and professional groups; labor leaders; small business owners; and manufacturers.

Title Five of the constitution officially defines the *loya jirga's* mission, duties, responsibilities, and structure:[3]

> *Article 78 The Loya Jirga (Great Council) consists of members of the Shura (Parliament) and the Chairmen of the Provincial Councils.*
>
> *In the event of the dissolution of the Shura (Parliament) its members retain their position as members of the Loya Jirga (Great Council) until a new Shura (Parliament) comes into being.*
>
> *Article 79 Subject to the provisions of Articles 19, 21 and 22 of this Constitution, the Loya Jirga (Great Council) is summoned by a Royal proclamation.[4]*
>
> *Article 80 When the Loya Jirga (Great Council) is in session, the provisions of Article 51 are applicable to its members.[5]*
>
> *Article 81 The deliberations of the Loya Jirga (Great Council) are open unless the Government or at least twenty members of the Loya Jirga (Great Council) request a secret session and the Loya Jirga (Great Council) approves this request.*
>
> *Article 82 The President of the Wolesi Jirga (House of the People), and in his absence, the President of the Meshrano Jirga (House of the Elders) presides over the Loya Jirga (Great Council).*
>
> *The Loya Jirga (Great Council), at its first meeting, elects one of its members as Secretary.*

Article 83 Except in cases clearly defined in this Constitution, the deci-sions of the Loyal Jirga (Great Council) shall be by a majority of the votes of its members present.

The procedure of the Loya Jirga (Great Council) shall be regulated by law, subject to the provisions of this Constitution.

Article 84 The Loya Jirga (Great Council) enjoys the powers defined in this Constitution.

The 1964 constitution enabled the country to move steadily toward a parliamentary system and the separation of powers. It also guaranteed freedom of expression and the right of women to be equal partners with men. One result was that Kabul University, a coeducational institution, would provide the country with women doctors, judges, professors, and political leaders. Women won seats in the house of representatives and the senate. Three women were appointed to the cabinet. Article 21 of the constitution even allowed the rule of a queen as regent.[6]

In the cities, women and men worked together in every sector of the society, from factories and beauty shops to judicial courts and univer-sities. In rural areas, they took care of their farms and livestock together. In other words, the impediments to women's intellectual and profes-sional growth, which had troubled Afghanistan to a greater or lesser de-gree for centuries, were disappearing.

In 1977 Mohammed Daoud, who had come to power by a coup d'état, convened a *loya jirga* to elect the next president of Afghanistan for a five-year-term. Mohammed Daoud himself was elected. Unfortu-nately, he did not complete his term due to the Communist coup; he was assassinated in 1978.

The Communist government attempted to legitimize the Soviet oc-cupation through the use of a *loya jirga* in 1987. While they were suc-cessful in formulating a new constitution and electing Dr. Mohammed Najibullah as president, they were unsuccessful in appeasing the Afghan people or overcoming their resistance to Communism. In fact, on September 27, 1996, "Afghanistan's Taliban militia seized control of Kabul soon after government forces abandoned the shattered Afghan capital. In its first action, the Islamic militant group hanged former

President Najibullah and his brother from a tower. . . . Crowds of Afghans cheered at the sight of Najibullah's beaten and bloated body hanging outside the presidential palace."[7]

Whether or not the *loya jirga* is always viable, it is very important to the people of Afghanistan. It is acceptable to all ethnic groups because it is a result-oriented process. It has always striven to bring peace to disputing groups and helped Afghans deal with chaotic situations and emergencies.

THE ROLE OF THE *LOYA JIRGA* IN THE TWENTY-FIRST CENTURY

Afghanistan has been struggling to preserve its independence since 1747, when Ahmad Shah Durrani liberated the Pashtun tribes from Persian domination. *Jirgas* and *loya jirgas* were the primary instruments in this struggle. The delegates to the Bonn meetings in 2001 were paying attention to history when they decreed that at the end of a six-month interim government, a *loya jirga,* inclusive of women as well as "all ethnic and religious groups and sects," would be convened to determine the composition of the eighteen-month transitional government before the Afghan people elect their permanent government in 2003. Article 3 of the procedures for the elections of the members of the Emergency *Loya Jirga* states:

> The Emergency Loya Jirga shall be held, based on the Bonn Agreement, with the purpose of ensuring the inherent right of the people, in freely determining their political destiny, based on the principles of Islam, restoration of peace, national reconciliation, the respect of human rights in the country, strengthening of independence, national sovereignty, territorial integrity, democracy, pluralism, and social justice.[8]

WOMEN'S RIGHTS

Under the leadership of King Mohammad Zahir Shah, programs of liberalization in Afghanistan addressed the importance of women's roles in society. Unfortunately, the Communist regime and then the fundamentalists brought an end to this process. Now, in the twenty-first century, women's freedom in Afghanistan is still as basic an issue as it was in 1919 when King Amanollah Shah began to integrate women's emancipation into his policies.

Article 3, which sets forth the agenda of the future government, does not place the women's issue on a long list of social problems to be solved. Rather, women are impacted by and can be part of the solution to every social problem. Without women's full participation in all aspects of reconstruction, the process may not be successful and peace may not return to Afghanistan. To restore democracy to Afghanistan, women must be guaranteed constitutional rights, social freedom, and freedom of choice. As important as the formation of a *loya jirga* is to the recovery of Afghanistan, the presence of women as representatives is even more crucial. Only with their participation will Afghans have the opportunity to reestablish a civil society without discrimination. It is my great hope not only that Afghans achieve this goal but also that our achievement will serve as an inspiration and a model for the many countries in the world where women are deprived of human rights.

The struggle the Afghan people have endured both within and outside the country is not an isolated historical event but one that has been orchestrated by many world players. Only now that the damage has reached beyond Afghanistan's borders is the international community ready to help. The only way that Afghanistan can take the next step into the future is through a globally supported *loya jirga*.

Notes

1. A violent ruler who freed Persia from the Afghans in 1729 and declared himself king. In 1738 he invaded Kandahar and captured Kabul.
2. On Amanollah and the revolts against him, see Leon B. Poullada, *Reform and Rebellion in Afghanistan, 1919–1929: King Amanullah's Failure to Modernize a Tribal Society* (Ithaca, NY: Cornell University Press, 1973);

Louis Dupree, *Afghanistan* (Princeton, NJ: Princeton University Press, 1973); Vartan Gregorian, *The Emergence of Modern Afghanistan: Politics of Reform and Modernization, 1880–1946* (Stanford, CA: Stanford University Press, 1969); and *A History of Afghanistan,* trans. Vitaly Baskakov (Moscow: Progress Publishers, 1985).

3. Constitution of Afghanistan, 9 Mizan 1343 (lunar calendar), October 1, 1964. This is the official English version published in Afghanistan.

4. Article 79: Whenever the King abdicates or dies without a son possessing the qualifications to become the King, the Throne shall pass on to the oldest of the King's brothers.

In case the oldest of the King's brothers lacks the qualifications needed, the Throne shall pass on to the second brother in line and so on.

If the King does not have a brother possessing the qualifications required for the King, his successor shall be elected from amongst the male-lineal descendants of His Majesty Mohammed Nadir Shah, the Martyr. In this case the King shall be elected by an Electoral College consisting of the Loya Jirgah (Great Council), the Government, and the Justices of the Supreme Court. This Electoral College shall be summoned by the Prime Minister, in the case of the death of the King within fifteen days from the date of the demise and in the case of abdication within seven days from the date when the King's abdication becomes effective. The decision of this Electoral College shall be by a majority of votes of the members present and shall be considered effective upon the consent of the person chosen as the King.

The Minister of Court shall act as Regent from the time of the death of the King or the validation of his abdication until the election of his successor.

5. Article 51: No legal proceedings can be brought against a member of the Shura (Parliament) for expressing an opinion or idea while performing his duty inside or outside the Shura (Parliament).

Whenever a member of the Shura (Parliament) is accused of an offence, the official responsible shall communicate the matter to the House of which the accused is a member. The legal proceedings against the accused shall be initiated when the House votes its approval by a two-thirds majority of its members. The House can also rescind its permission by a two-thirds majority vote of its members.

In the case of a witnessed crime the official responsible can start legal proceedings and arrest a member of the Shura (Parliament) without the permission of the House to which he belongs.

Whenever legal proceedings demand the detention of the accused in accordance with the provisions of the law, the official responsible is bound to communicate the matter immediately to the House concerned, and with its permission may detain the accused. In case the accusation occurs during the period when the House is not in session, permission for detention shall be obtained from the Executive Council of the House. The decision of the Executive Council shall be placed before the House at its next session for appropriate action.

6. Article 21: In case the King dies before his successor has completed twenty years of life, the Queen shall act as Regent until his successor reaches the stipulated age.

7. See *http://www.cnn.com/WORLD/9609/27/afghan.rebels/*

8. For the full text of this document, see *http://un.org.pk/latest-dev/key-doc-loyerjirga.htm*

A VISION OF JUSTICE, EQUALITY, AND PEACE

FAHIMA VORGETTS

I HAVE A VISION for Afghanistan. It has been with me ever since I was a little girl, and while it has grown and matured into something politically sound and spiritually grounded, it retains its childlike simplicity.

I envision a country in which men and women are equal in every aspect of their lives—education, employment, marriage, politics, and society—and a world in which all human beings are allowed freedom of choice in religion and lifestyle. Everyone lives together in peace.

As a child I gazed at a family and a society filled with injustice, especially toward women. I was born in 1954 and grew up in a traditional Afghan extended family that consisted not only of my parents and siblings, but also of many aunts, uncles, cousins, and other relatives living in our home. Throughout my childhood I had ample opportunity to observe the way men and women related to each other, and what I saw was very disturbing.

The women were expected to do all the housework, while the men either went to work or lounged around. Women waited on men hand and foot. A woman had to ask her male relative for permission for everything, even to leave the house. Men were allowed to take more than one wife, while a woman could have only one husband. I personally knew several polygamous men and their families. Not surprising, rivalry among the wives was common, and their situation caused them great suffering. It was a custom guaranteed to humiliate them. Many women were forced into marriages they did not want, and in marriage they were expected to be submissive to their husbands. When a woman's husband died, she was expected to obey her son, who then became the new head of the household.

From the age of five or six, I was initiated into the responsibilities of cooking and taking care of younger siblings. So were my female cousins, sisters, and friends. But my brothers and male cousins had no such responsibilities. What child wants to work while other children are playing? But it was not just the extra work that distressed me; I resented the inequity. I was filled with moral outrage. It made no sense. If God had created all human beings, then surely all human beings were equal. Men had no intrinsic superiority over women, and it was not fair that they were accorded such privilege.

When I took my questions to the adults in my life, I got an unsatisfactory response: This is how things have always been, and there is nothing anyone can do about it. Moreover, I was often given the religious explanation that this is what the Qur'an teaches and what God wants. Then they would say, "Stop asking these disrespectful questions and finish washing the dishes!"

Whenever I heard these things, I would become furious. I resented the adults for shoving religion down my throat, and I resented what religion did to women.

As I grew older, I started to wonder whether other people were as angry and resentful as I was. I asked my friends about their households and families. Were they also being discriminated against, and how did they feel about it? As we shared our stories, we realized that we all felt the same way. We began to discuss how we could bring about changes. We began to read books together. The timing of our unrest was perfect. This was a time of political change in Afghanistan.

Policy regarding women had vacillated between the extremely conservative and the more progressive throughout the twentieth century. In 1959, Prime Minister Daoud Khan and senior members of his government shocked everyone by appearing in public with their wives and daughters—and the women were not wearing scarves or veils! Soon, women began to enter the workforce. The new Constitutional Advisory Committee created by King Zahir Shah in 1964 included two women. One of the most important aspects of the new Constitution was that it gave legal equality to men and women. It also stated that although Islam was the sacred religion of Afghanistan, the secular legal system would take precedence over *shariya* (Islamic law). Finally, it called for a democratic process—an elected parliament.

The first parliamentary election changed my life. For the first time, women could play a role in government and in the future of the country. In fact, that first parliament, elected in 1965, had four female members. Although 4 out of 216 was a tiny percentage (1.85 percent), it was a big accomplishment.

At this time, a new organization called the Women's Democratic Organization (WDO) was forming. Even though I was only ten years old, I helped in its formation. By the time I was thirteen I was a full member, attending meetings without the knowledge of my family. Needless to say, this organization did not go over very well with the oppressive society. No one would support it—no one, that is, except the Communists, who saw their support as a way of gaining the allegiance of a whole new group of people, the women. The women, in turn, were happy to have the validation of the Communists. And, of course, there were some points of similarity, at least in theory, between the women's rights movement and the Communist movement. Both believed in equality for all people and freedom from oppression.

At the WDO, my friends and I found a supportive environment of like-minded women, and we no longer felt alone. Unfortunately, though, our involvement with the WDO created problems at home. Traditional families tended to oppose any movement that challenged the status quo. We all had to struggle for our beliefs, but the struggle only brought us closer and increased our commitment.

During the fifteen years I was involved in WDO (I left Afghanistan in 1979), I learned a lot about the inner workings of an organization—especially how to create a grassroots movement. Change *must* take place at a grassroots level. It cannot be imposed from above.

Keeping this concept at the fore, we tackled as our first issue education for women and girls. We worked in the community, trying to persuade women and their fathers and husbands that everybody has the right to education. We quoted verses from the Qur'an that praise the value of reading scripture and allude to the importance of education for both sexes. This approach was effective. Many previously apprehensive men were willing to allow their wives and daughters to be educated, and women in turn were eager to learn.

The members of the Soviet-backed government were largely Afghan, and their methods were radically different from the WDO's. One of the ongoing disagreements WDO had with the Communists' approach to education was their dogmatism. They did not adapt their vision to the realities and values of the vast majority of Afghans. The government attempted to fast-forward all sorts of major societal changes the people simply were not ready for. This created resentment among the fierce, proud Afghans.

My colleagues and I were especially disturbed by their approach to education. Teachers were sent to rural areas where there were high rates of illiteracy, especially among women. They often arranged classes in peoples' homes, and the local authorities forced women and their daughters to attend. Many Afghans saw these trends as a threat to their family life and their identity. Education became associated with humiliation, foreign domination, and everything that was un-Islamic and anti-Islamic.

I once believed communism was the road to fulfilling the vision I had as a child. Instead, communism turned out to be another coercive system. I was profoundly disillusioned, and I learned a hard lesson. Fanaticism is not confined to religious people. Anyone who is dogmatic about his or her beliefs, seeks to impose those beliefs on others, and refuses to hear another point of view is a fanatic.

In rebellion, many angry tribes united to form the mujahideen, who set out to liberate Afghanistan from foreign rule and reclaim it as an Islamic country. The mujahideen were motivated by the Islamic concept of a jihad or holy war. In fact, the word "mujahideen" means "people of jihad." This started one of the darkest, bloodiest periods in Afghan history, when the United States and the Soviet Union used Afghanistan as an arena for their war games. The United States supplied the mujahideen with weapons and encouraged the Islamization of the war.

The mujahideen did more than fight the Soviets. They fought other Afghans. "Fought" is too gentle a term; "butchered" is more accurate. They killed Afghan people who they claimed had been influenced by communism. This included government employees, people with higher education, and working women. I do not know a single family that was unaffected.

During those years, women's education came to a halt. Women were raped, tortured, and killed by the mujahideen. Any work for women's rights had to be relegated to the back burner because day-to-day survival became the most important priority. Then, once the Taliban assumed power in 1995, women's education was forced to go underground, since the Taliban outlawed it altogether. All the hard work the women's rights organizations had put into women's education was undone.

Now the Taliban have been overthrown, and we are poised for change. This can be a time of growth and opportunity for women—if it is handled correctly. Above all, we must not forget the lessons of the past in the urgency of the moment. In my opinion, these five steps are necessary:

1. *Start with disarmament.* The massive influx of weapons into Afghanistan has created a situation in which almost every man is armed. I believe it is impossible to work for peace when there are weapons in every household—especially among a population with such a long history of violence.

2. *Create a secular government.* I believe a secular government is essential if equality, freedom, and justice are to prevail in any society. The periods when Afghan women enjoyed the greatest opportunity coincided with governments that did not adhere rigidly to religious law—first in the 1920s under King Amanollah Shah, then in the 1960s under King Zahir Shah, and finally under the Communists in the 1980s.

A secular government is more likely to respect each person's right to his or her religion because it is not allied with any particular religious system. Furthermore, a secular government will protect people from religious fanaticism.

But the world must accept and respect that a secular government in Afghanistan today may not resemble secular governments in other parts of the world because of how deeply embedded religion is in our culture. The people of Afghanistan must be allowed and enabled to create a just and healthy nation on their own terms.

3. *Educate, educate, educate.* A secular government is an important beginning, but it is not enough. Even the secular legal system mandated by King Zahir Shah was not sufficient to create deep and lasting change within society. The new constitution gave equal rights to everyone, but culture and society did not follow suit. That was very shattering for me. I sincerely believed that within five or ten years, complete equality would be achieved. Now I understand that my ideas were not realistic. Since change cannot be imposed externally but must spring from hearts of the population, it is a process that will take much longer than five or ten years. Such profound change in Afghanistan will require decades of careful education and consciousness-raising to take root.

It is a well-known fact that Afghanistan had an elite urban class in the 1960s onward who were highly educated—so the notion of a world-class education is not alien to us. In the new

Afghanistan, education must transcend mere literacy and be accessible to all in the country. If we fail at this, Afghanistan will remain vulnerable to the anti-modern fundamentalists who are responsible for so much of the country's tortured history.

The system of education must provide exposure not only to ideas but also to practical knowledge and skills. When people have marketable skills and can earn a decent living, they gain self-respect. And when they have some hope that their work will lead to an improved quality of life and that the rewards of the modern world are not permanently beyond their means or their children's, they will be less likely to resort to the "-isms" that have brought their country down: warlordism, fanaticism, terrorism.

In the case of women, education can suggest that the submissive role they have been taught to play is not inevitable. The importance of acquiring a profession or at least a set of skills they can use in order to be economically independent cannot be emphasized enough. When a woman is dependent upon her husband for food, clothing, and shelter, her choices are severely limited. She must endure whatever he does to her, including physical abuse. A woman who is self-sustaining has a much wider range of choices.

Ultimately the need for education applies to both women and men. The more men are educated, the more they will support the education of their wives and daughters.

An important segment of the children's population has special educational and social needs. Children, war orphans in particular, have typically ended up being educated at the *madressas* in Pakistan. These Islamic schools are known for their indoctrination of young boys, who are taught that their purpose in life is to wage a *jihad*. *Madressas* thrive because they are free and provide meals; poor families have no option but to send their children there. Orphanages offering support services and a secular curriculum, or at least a moderate and respectful Islamic curriculum, will help ensure that we do not raise a new generation of terrorists.

Education and exposure to ideas through all available means will enable the people of Afghanistan to re-imagine and actualize an alternative to a culture of violence and oppression.

4. *Find peaceful solutions.* Remedying the social circumstances, such as poverty and ignorance, that have led religious extremists in Afghanistan to violence and terrorism will be far more valuable than bombing them.

Mediation is a powerful tool for bringing peace, not only among individuals but also among tribes, factions, and even nations. Many if not most Afghans have never been taught some of the most basic communication skills. Mediation and dialogue skills will help men and women, different ethnicities, political factions, and ultimately nations resolve conflict peaceably.

5. *Take it step by step.* Social change in Afghanistan will occur person by person. The person who learns to read; the woman who starts to work; the man who starts to regard his wife with more respect—each is a step toward a confident people and a strong and enduring nation. And so, over a period of decades, transformation of individuals will result in deep and radical societal change. This time, they will not be changes imposed by a government but changes that arise from within the hearts of people themselves.

During 2002 I have been collecting textbooks and supplies for Kabul University and other universities and schools in Afghanistan, where entire libraries were burnt down by the fundamentalists. I visited Afghanistan earlier this year and came across more than fifteen new women's organizations and projects that gave me great hope and inspiration. I have been fundraising for these small and large grassroots initiatives by touring the United States doing speaking engagements. I believe that if the schools and universities can begin to educate my people, and the women of my country are supported in their efforts to empower their sisters and advocate for women's rights, the vision I had as a child, of an Afghanistan of peace and gender equity, will be within reach.

MISS AFGHANISTAN

A Story of a Nation

Zohra Yusuf Daoud

With contributions from Murwarid Abdiani

LET'S TELL A STORY, a story about a different time. More specifically, let's tell a story about the women of a now-downtrodden nation, struggling to rise above a nearly irreversible state of chaos and rebuild their country. For a time these women were hidden away from the world and were covered from head to toe. Unable to leave their homes, they were locked away like possessions.

We can now see them on our televisions in news reports. For an American to see such an image must be a foreign experience. Never do we see women in the United States walking around in *burqas,* covered from head to toe, beaten for showing a little skin or walking among men. But perhaps what Americans don't know is that for an Afghan to see such an image is also strange. Contrary to what you may think, and contrary to what you may have heard about Islam or Afghanistan, this treatment of women is not native to my culture. This is not Afghanistan's Islam.

Over the centuries, there have been revolutions, there have been movements for freedom and equality, there have been struggles and sacrifices the world over. People have given the most valuable commodity they lay claim to—their lives—to create change and protect freedom. The Berlin Wall came down. Communism was defeated. Apartheid came to an end. We sought resolution in Bosnia. But the women of Afghanistan were overlooked. Somehow those who could protect turned into those who would oppress. In doing so, they infected the fabric of a society with disillusionment and hopelessness.

Unbeknownst to most of the world, Afghanistan was once an Islamic Paris, an enlightened country, with European and Asian influences and diverse ethnicities and tribal cultures. Our legacy ran deep, as did our historical and geographical significance on the continent. We were a small country, but a country working to empower itself through universal education.

Once, before the Soviet invasion in 1979, women had rights in Afghanistan. They were treated like human beings. Once women were a productive part of society in Afghanistan, helping the nation grow. There was a time when women worked side by side with men in the fields just as there was a time when they worked side by side with men in parliament and in universities. Women once had a voice in Afghanistan; they were heard and acknowledged.

But to say that all women in Afghanistan had as much freedom as women in the United States would be incorrect. More accurately, the only the privileged few, sprinkled throughout the urban areas of Afghanistan, gained these freedoms. Unfortunately, the rural areas of Afghanistan were rarely in step with the rest of the country. This reality we must acknowledge, that even before 1979, there was not total equality for all women. But we were working toward that goal and making progress.

I know this because I was there. I was a part of that change. I am one of that fortunate minority of women who were modernized and educated in Afghanistan. I grew up in Kabul and led a reasonably charmed life. My father was a Columbia University graduate, a doctor, and Afghanistan's surgeon general. We were a well-off family. We were the kind of family that spent nine months of the year living in one home and the winter months in another simply because we could afford to escape the cold. I had three brothers and five sisters, which by Afghan standards was average. What was not the norm was the fact that my father encouraged us all to pursue higher education. And by all of us, what I really mean is all of his girls. My father taught us that in Islam it is written that all men and women have the right to knowledge, that it is their duty as human beings to educate and to be educated. In my family, this belief was practiced.

The thirst for knowledge that my father fostered led me into one of the sweetest experiences of my life. In 1972 something as simple as a beauty pageant would forever change me. I was crowned the first ever "Miss Afghanistan." There was, of course, no swimsuit competition and no emphasis on beauty; to be perfectly honest, I was even a little chubby then. Instead, the pageant was about a woman's intellect and poise. It was about public speaking and academic knowledge. More than anything, however, this pageant was about progress. In America, pageants seem to be trivial events that have had feminists up in arms and perhaps rightly so. In Afghanistan, however, a pageant meant we were catching up to the world, working to fit in, joining the global community. It meant we were moving forward, moving away from archaic notions and toward a balanced modernization.

Standing there with the other finalists, palms sweaty and nervous as hell, I had no idea how my life was about to change. But there I was, the first and, unbeknownst to me, the only Miss Afghanistan. As the winner, I was afforded the opportunity to travel to big cities like Herat, Mazaar-e-Sharif, and Kandahar to fulfill my responsibility as Miss Afghanistan: to promote the country's literacy program in areas where there was little encouragement to get an education. Part of this outreach meant visiting women's prisons in Afghanistan. It was there that

I witnessed the few things that would change me the most as a young woman.

The jails were full of women. Some of them had run away from forced marriages. Others were in prison for killing husbands who had beaten them severely, while many had merely run away from domestic abuse. None of these women was allowed to seek a divorce, none could return to her family. My heart sank with the weight of what I was witnessing. The plight of these women, their oppression and sadness, was very un-Islamic and very disappointing in a nation that had worked hard to join the modern world. In these rural areas I encountered explosive mixtures of religion and culture. I learned that there were places in Afghanistan where men and women did not stand on equal ground. There were tribal cultures that denied women an education because they deemed it unnecessary, and even some that considered brutality against women normal.

This was a stark contrast to my own experience. In Kabul, I had taken equality between men and women for granted with respect to religion, culture, and law. I was the daughter of a mother who had never worn a veil. I attended coed universities where male and female professors taught side by side and respected each other's accomplishments. I wore blue jeans and sunglasses. When it came time to marry, my father left the choice of a suitor to me. In Kabul theaters women acted on stage before the public. We had radio personalities and women provided voices. We had female singers, female flight attendants, and saleswomen who assisted men in department stores. We had women writers who contributed to, as well as published, magazines. We had women in politics; we even had anchorwomen on television's national news.

I resolved to follow the lead of these women and parlay my success in the beauty pageant into something important for myself. Being a part of the literacy campaign opened my eyes to the deficiencies of my country, and I yearned to beat the odds. Traveling to distant communities where equality was not a possibility, far less a priority, I worked hard to find my place as a woman in Afghanistan. I wanted to follow role models who preceded me. I hoped to become a role model for all the women in those prisons and for all the little girls who dared to dream of a fuller life for themselves.

I became one of the voices of Afghanistan. I became a news anchor and a radio personality, and I even spent a few years translating French news periodicals into Dari (classical Farsi, one of the two most commonly spoken languages in Afghanistan) for news agencies in Kabul. I came from a prominent family, but I made a name for myself based on my work.

But I must repeat that not every woman in Afghanistan had these opportunities. Women in Afghanistan had come very far, but we needed to keep moving ahead. Although all women had the right to vote, not all women were allowed to exercise this right. Although theoretically women had the choice not to wear a veil, not all women were permitted to make that choice. Although theoretically every Afghan woman had a chance at an education, not all women could seize that precious opportunity. Islam wasn't keeping these women from moving forward; the traditionalists and their cultures were women's greatest obstacles in their quest for equality. It was patriarchy, threatened by the prospect of women's empowerment, that hindered women's use of their legal rights.

This perceived threat has remained the central detriment to Afghanistan's progress. Historically, change and modernization have always been challenged in that country. Traditionalists, empowered by religious zealots, have always managed to stop progress in its tracks, to throw a hammer into the gears of an evolving democratic society. Afghanistan's track record in the area of women's rights is long and often reads like a multiple bell curve. Reforms started as far back as the 1880s, when Amir Abdor Rahman Khan raised the age of marriage, which ended the practice of child brides. These reforms gave women the right to divorce under secular law. In 1909 progress continued with King Habibollah Shah, who allowed his wives to abandon the traditional veil and appear publicly in Western clothes. In 1919 his son King

Amanollah ascended the throne, and he and his wife, Queen Soraya, brought enlightenment and further progress to Afghanistan. The king gave all women the option to remove the veil, a garment not like the all-encompassing *burqas* we see today, but a traditional veil that covers only the wearer's head. He opened a number of schools in 1921; I am an alumna of one of them. He sent women to Europe to receive their advanced education; he and the queen both received honorary degrees from Oxford University.

When these monumental changes were taking place, the traditionalists became increasingly agitated. Kings of the late nineteenth and early twentieth centuries defended their progressive decisions, citing the Qur'an as the basis for changing laws. They emphasized that they were allowing women rights already accorded them in the Qur'an. Later, presidents defended these decisions, emphasizing that Afghan women were crucial to the economy. If there were women professors and physicians, they said, the embarrassment most women felt about being educated and receiving healthcare would be reduced significantly. Unfortunately, since the onslaught of the wars in Afghanistan, most of those rights and protections have been withdrawn.

Queen Soraya sounds like an early feminist in her address to a group of women on Afghanistan's seventh independence anniversary in 1926: "Do not think . . . that our nation needs only men to serve it. Women should also take their part as women did in the early years of Islam. The valuable services rendered by women are recounted throughout history from which we learn that women were not created solely for pleasure and comfort. From their examples we learn that we must all contribute toward the development of our nation and that this can not be done without being equipped with knowledge."[1]

The surge of progress was palpable. Gradually women were included in most areas of public society. In the 1950s Afghanistan's women were called to action in the workforce by the government. In 1959 women became economically active and worked with men to reach development goals for the country. In the 1960s women were granted increasingly equal rights. In 1964 women were constitutionally allowed to join the government and vote. The year 1965 brought about the formation of the Women's Democratic Organization, a group dedicated to eliminating illiteracy among women and to banning forced marriages. The members of this organization are now scattered around the world. In the 1970s women began adopting Western styles of dress, and by 1979 a full 50 percent of college students, government workers, and teachers in Afghanistan were women.

When war came to Afghanistan, all that magnificent progress came to a standstill. War steals the very breath that life offers, and Afghanistan stopped breathing. For twenty-two years, my homeland has been dead. Learning nothing from history, the world chose to turn the other cheek, ignoring the wars, the famines, the refugee crises, and the degradation of an entire population of women. Now, post September 11, we are all working diligently to breathe life back into what has become a killing field. To accomplish this resuscitation, we must also breathe life back into the mothers and daughters of a generation forgotten, into those who will carry a nation and nurse it back to health.

How do we create a future for women in Afghanistan? Indeed, how do we create a foundation without fear? How do we move forward a nation of women immobilized by years of immeasurable psychological conditioning? It is foolish to believe that when the Taliban in Kabul were toppled, all the women ran into the streets and flung off their *burqas.* Or to think that most women are leaving their homes and exploring the streets outside their blackened windows. And it is imprudent to believe that after years of conditioning by the Taliban, Afghan men would allow women these liberties in the first place. For some women perhaps, these choices have become cultural. They will continue to wear the *burqa,* they will continue to stay at home, excluding themselves from the company of men and society. Others will do so out of fear. Years of beatings and beratings, not only from the Taliban but also from their own family members, will have "convinced" many women that their proper place is not in society.

To find a hero or a staunch advocate of women's rights in Afghanistan will be quite a feat. Women's rights have not been on the agenda in Afghanistan for the past twenty-two years, during which time Afghanistan's wives and daughters have been deprived of the most important tools for survival: healthcare and education. The price they are paying is evident in the psychological and physical damage we witness on our television screens nightly. Many women have opted for the freedom that death offers; suicide is the only option they believe they have. We must change that. We need to help them heal, to involve them in their nation's affairs, to involve them in the families they run, and to embrace them once again in the world of the living.

But care must be taken. Before women can run, they must learn to walk again. Some aspects associated with Western feminism, such as bra-burning, revealing clothing, and sexual promiscuity are not appropriate at this stage for Afghan feminists, if they ever will be. The first step must be to restore to women their basic human rights. There must be a fair balance of religion, culture, and law. And Afghan women must be protected in order to survive, to imagine and plan a future for themselves and the generations to come. Without rights and protections, they will be dead to the world, just as they were prior to September 11.

When women once again possess the gifts of life and knowledge, they will become teachers and they will teach their children well. Teaching has always been an honorable profession in Afghanistan. But while an Afghan father does well when he teaches his son to pick up a rifle and defend his country, women will teach an entire generation what it has not had the opportunity to learn: the literacy of peace.

By ensuring Afghan women an education, we will do double duty. Not only is it critical to their survival and to the immediate rebuilding of Afghanistan, but it will also provide future generations of women with powerful role models. All we have to do is look inside Afghanistan to see the immense costs of ignorance. Look at the illiterate orphans, easily brainwashed because they have been forced to memorize religious texts in a language they neither read nor understand. The lessons of humanity that are intended by those words are being kept from them. The consequence of this deadening of young Muslim minds was September 11. Take into account that women accept beatings as a way of life simply because their mullahs have told them the Qur'an gives their husbands the right. If these women possessed the ability to read, they would have found the protections their religion provides them. Perhaps they might have questioned what was happening to them. When we stop learning, we stop inquiring; when the Taliban deprived women of education, they took away a their rights to question and to effect change.

I'm no politician, I'm no activist. I am a mother, a wife, a woman, and a refugee from a country whose glory has long since passed. Like so many other Americans, I am an immigrant with only stories of what my life used to be like in a land far away. My children have a nice home, my husband works hard; I have a fine family. But watching the news every night, I cry over rubbled streets that were once my playgrounds. I cry over children who have no homes, no mothers, and no fathers. I weep over seven-year-old boys who carry guns and over teenage girls who have been raped. I shed tears for the lack of color in my once-ornate homeland, watching as nothing but dirt sweeps by the television cameras. I am saddened that Americans think Afghanistan has always been like this. So I speak out about what I know and how I lived when I was there.

For years the fact that I was Miss Afghanistan was just a memory I stored in a box. Just good old times my friends and I could laugh about. Now it has become a blessed platform. I can only hope that by telling my story every chance I get, I become an example for some young Afghan girl. Maybe if she knew that once, long ago, her wartorn country was a paradise, she'd work hard to make it that paradise again. This is my true hope for Afghanistan, my hope for the young women there who will one day deliver a nation by standing tall and never again falling victim to atrocity.

Maybe then something as silly as a beauty pageant will change someone else's life, the way it changed mine.

NOTES

1. Louis Dupree, *Afghanistan* (Princeton, NJ; Princeton University Press, 1986).

HISTORY, FACES, TRANSPLANTED LIVES

LINA PALLOTTA

1. Roya Ghiasy (left) Lida Ahmady (foreground) and Women for Afghan Women (WAW) board member Zolaykha Sherzad (right) at Chuk Palu, an Afghan store on 5th Ave. NYC, January 2002. ©Lina Pallotta.

2. Catherine Papell of the Universalist Church of Flushing embracing Sabera Noori, a member of the Queens Outreach Group of WAW, after a special interfaith service held at the church. WAW board member Marti Copleman and program coordinator Masuda Sultan are in the background. NYC, February 24, 2002. ©Lina Pallotta.

3. Roya Ghiasy (right), Lida Ahmady (left), and Naheed Elyasi (center)at Chuk Palu. NYC, January 2002. © Lina Pallotta.

4. Mariam Mamoor showing her henna-painted hand during the celebration of the end of Ramadan at her grandparents' house. Her sister Rubina is seen at her side. Long Island, December 16, 2001.©Lina Pallotta.

5. Zolaykha Sherzad. NYC, January 2002. ©Lina Pallotta.

6. Latifa Woodhouse Yusufi, WAW member, at the Newton High School in Queens where she teaches English. NYC, February 14, 2002. ©Lina Pallotta.

7. Freshta Amirzada, WAW member, at Queens College. NYC, February 2002. ©Lina Pallotta

8. Fariba Nawa on the roof of her apartment building in Brooklyn looking where the WTC used to be. NYC, February 2002. ©Lina Pallotta.

9. WAW board member Homaira Mamoor and her daughter Rubina praying at the Islamic Center of Long Island. February 2002. ©Lina Pallotta.

10. Rahim Walizada and his friend Lida Ahmady at Chuk Palu. NYC, January 2002. ©Lina Pallotta.

11. Masuda Mamoor and her husband Abdullah Mamoor in their house on Long Island. December 2001. ©Lina Pallotta.

12. WAW board member Afifa Yusufi walking towards Homayra Amirzada and her twin sister Freshta Amirzada (right) at Queens College. They are members of the Queens Outreach Committee of WAW. NYC, February 2002. ©Lina Pallotta.

13. Zohra Rasekh of Global Watch Group at WAW conference. November 2001. ©Lina Pallotta.

14. Wazhmah Osman, WAW board member. NYC, February 2002. ©Lina Pallotta.

15. Sunita Mehta, WAW co-founder, at WAW conference. NYC, November 2001. ©Lina Pallotta.

16. Homaira Mamoor praying at the Islamic Center of Long Island. February 2002.© Lina Pallotta.

17. Leeza Ahmady dancing at Chuk Palu. NYC, February 2002. ©Lina Pallotta.

Section Two

*Stories and Strategies
for Claiming the Future*

In Mourning of My City

ATIA GAHEEZ

Like the sorrowed tears of a mother's eyes
That fall on a body sleeping in a coffin
That day the sun was shining kindly
On the ruined walls of my city
When I stepped through the huge gate
The wind sent me a Hello
Full with dust

The stone walls bent along my way
As if I had a message from a new life
My poor city does not know that
I left it in the claws of adversity
I broke my relation with it
So the dust of its sorrow does not catch me

When I stepped farther
I felt a sting inside me
Although silence was ruling everywhere
The bitter scream of the broken walls
Shook me from head to foot

A scream rose from the broken bones of the houses
Saying that hopes are lost
Satan put the crown of a kingdom on
Even the rubble is sentenced with slavery
The silent scream of rubble said that

Everywhere is filled with the sound and color of
    mourning
The earth has changed to a cemetery of humans and
    their wishes

The faces of living beings are mirrors of sorrow
Hearts empty from the light of hope for a tomorrow
Every lip has the story of hatred
The smoke of night is
Running in the heart of days
With haste
Eyes are full of blood from
Fear and trepidation

O God, why did the altar of hopes of my city's
    bride break?
Her white dress covered in red blood
And the sorrowed tears washed her beautiful face

Every heart that has this sorrow says that
My beautiful city has gone to waste
A devil broke into it and
Spread the poison of discord
My beautiful city became
A victim of an aimless war

—translated from Persian by the author

Faryad *(Scream)*

ATIA GAHEEZ

O man
O proud mortal
Leave me alone for a while with my own feelings
Let me out of this cold cage
Let me out of this painful prison
I have many unsaid sayings
I have a world of pain hidden in my heart
If you let me free
I will fly to the farthest skies
To the peak of mountains of light
With the wings of poetry
I will mix my voice with the swallows
And sing with them
And scream to the world
Of unloyal men
That I am a woman
Look toward me, toward us
As human beings

—translated from Persian by the author

ON MAKING POLITICAL CHANGE

RUTH MESSINGER

THERE IS NOTHING MORE IMPORTANT than the effort the women in this section are making to assert the rights of the women of Afghanistan, to insist that whatever work is being done to rebuild that country must include women as full participants. These women, each with their own experiences, are united on one point: that if Afghanistan is going to emerge from the oppressions of the Taliban and take its place in the twenty-first century, it must allow women to be part of the discussions, part of the planning, and full players in Afghan society and government.

And make no mistake about it. The women of Afghanistan have a tremendous amount to contribute to their own futures. From a distance I am privileged to know this as president of American Jewish World Service. For almost three years we have been supporting a group of Afghan women who organized to support seventy-five Afghan women teachers secretly running schools in their own homes, providing 2,500 Afghan girls with the tools they will need to take their rightful place in a liberated Afghanistan. Over time these women, displaying extraordinary bravery, ran schools, opened health clinics, set up programs and projects for Afghan women in the refugee camps in Pakistan, and showed just how able they were to plan for and implement social change. Their country will benefit greatly from freeing up the energies not only of these women but of all the women of a country in which women have for too long been victims.

This effort, then, is not only for the women of Afghanistan. It is for all the people of Afghanistan and the future of their country. It is not possible to build a modern nation on ostensibly democratic principles and to keep part of the nation subjugated. This effort is, also, for all of us. We have too few examples in the twenty-first century of people organizing to fight for their rights and, despite the progress made in many countries, not enough examples of women holding an equal place in their governments. We will all benefit from seeing what women in Afghanistan can do to take their rightful place in their country and change the future.

MUSLIM WOMEN'S RIGHTS

A CONTEMPORARY DEBATE

RIFFAT HASSAN

AMONG THE ISSUES that have come to the fore after the fall
of the Taliban in Afghanistan, none has attracted more world attention
than the situation of Afghan women. The Taliban imposed their own
distorted and brutal understanding of Islam upon Afghan women,
whose plight had been a matter of deep concern to a number of individuals and human rights organizations before September 11. Unfortunately, however, the victimization of women in Afghanistan, grave
as it was, was not an issue of such import for the United States or the
international community that military action would have been
launched to liberate these hapless human beings from unspeakable
tyranny.

The "liberation" of Afghan women from Taliban rule occurred as a
by-product of the U.S.-led military action in Afghanistan. If the events
of September 11 had not occurred, had not shaken the United States
and the international community, then I believe that Afghan women,
like countless others in situations of great pain and peril, would have
continued to live and die in horrific conditions under Taliban rule.

I do not know exactly when my "academic" study of women in Islam became a passionate quest for truth and justice on behalf of Muslim women—perhaps it was when I realized the impact on my own life of the so-called Islamic ideas and attitudes regarding women. What began as a scholarly exercise became simultaneously an Odyssean venture in self-understanding. But "enlightenment" does not always lead to "endless bliss" (in Buddhist terms). The more aware I became of the centrality of gender-justice and gender-equity in the Qur'anic teachings regarding women, the more troubled I felt seeing the injustice and inhumanity to which many Muslim women are subjected in actual life.

Despite the fact that women such as Khadijah and 'Ai'shah (wives of the Prophet Muhammad) and Rab'ia al-Basri (the outstanding woman Sufi) figured significantly in early Islam, the Islamic tradition has, by and large, remained rigidly patriarchal to this day. This means, among other things, that the sources on which this tradition is based, mainly the Qur'an (which Muslims believe to be God's Word transmitted through the Angel Gabriel to the Prophet Muhammad), *Sunnah* (the practice of the Prophet Muhammad), *Hadith* (the oral traditions attributed to the Prophet Muhammad), and *Fiqh* (jurisprudence), have been interpreted only by Muslim men, who have arrogated to themselves the task of defining the ontological, sociological, and eschatological status of Muslim women. It is hardly surprising that until now the majority of Muslim women, who have been kept for centuries in physical, mental, and emotional bondage, have accepted the situation passively. Here it needs to be mentioned that while the rate of literacy is low in many countries, the rate of literacy of Muslim women, especially those who live in rural areas, where most of the population lives, is among the lowest in the world.

While I have continued to pursue my theological research on issues relating to women in Islam, I have been increasingly engaged, since 1983, in sharing my research findings with diverse groups of Muslim women and youth in many countries. Believing that knowledge is power, I have endeavored, through travel and participation in educational meetings, to disseminate, particularly among Muslim women and girls, evidence of rights that are accorded to women in Islamic sources. I believe that given the centrality of religion to the lives of the vast majority of people in the Muslim world, the best way—if not the only way—to counteract the negative ideas and attitudes regarding females so widespread in the culture is by reference to the authority of the Qur'an or the ethical principles of normative Islam.

Following this principle, I have pursued research that demonstrates on the basis of an analysis of the Qur'anic text that the three assumptions on which the superstructure of the idea of man's superiority to woman has been erected, not only in the Islamic but also in the Jewish and Christian traditions, are unwarranted. Briefly put, these three assumptions are, first, that God's primary creation is man, not woman, since woman is believed to have been created from man's rib and is, therefore, derivative; second, that woman was the primary agent of "Man's Fall," and hence all "daughters of Eve" are to be regarded with hatred, suspicion, and contempt; and third, that woman was created not only from man but for man, which makes her existence merely instrumental.

In none of the thirty or so passages in the Qur'an that describe the creation of humanity is there any statement that supports the first assumption, that is, that asserts or suggests that man was created prior to woman or that woman was created from man. This means that the inequality of women and men in almost all Muslim (and many other) societies cannot be seen as having been willed by God, but must be seen as a perversion of God's intent in creation. Second, in the context of the story of the "Fall," the Qur'an provides no basis whatever for asserting or implying that Eve was tempted by Satan, in turn tempted and deceived Adam, and led to his expulsion from the Garden. Though no "Fall" occurs in the Qur'anic narrative and though there is no doctrine of Original Sin in Islam, patriarchal Muslim culture has used the Biblical myth to perpetuate the myth of feminine evil, particularly in order to control women's sexuality, which it associates, as does St. Augustine, with "fallenness." Third, the Qur'an does not support the view, held by many Muslims, Christians, and Jews, that woman was created not only *from* man, but also *for* man. Not only does the Qur'an make it clear that men and women stand absolutely equal in the sight of God, but they also are "members" and "protectors" of each other. In other words, the Qur'an does not create a hierarchy in which men are placed above women.

The United Nations International Conference on Population and Development (ICPD) held in Cairo, Egypt, in September 1994, was an extremely important landmark in raising global consciousness with regard to some of the most intimate and intricate issues pertaining to women's lives as well as human sexuality and relationships that have ever been discussed at an international forum. One of the fundamental issues underlying the deliberations of the Cairo conference was that of the "ownership" of a woman's body. Women's identification with body rather than with mind and spirit is a common characteristic of the dualistic thinking that pervades many religious, cultural, and philosophical traditions. Ironically, however, though women have traditionally been identified with body, they have not been seen as *owners* of their bodies, and the issue of who controls women's bodies—men, the state, the church, the community, or women—has never been decided in favor of women in patriarchal cultures. Muslim societies are far more concerned with trying to control women's bodies and sexuality than with granting women their human rights. When many Muslims speak of human rights, they either do not speak of women's rights at all, or they are concerned with how a woman's chastity may be protected. (They are apparently not worried about protecting men's chastity.)

The great breakthrough of the Cairo conference was the fact that Muslim women forcefully challenged the traditional viewpoint not only with regard to women's identification with body, but also with regard to the assumption that women are not *owners* of their bodies.

Having successfully challenged age-old definitions of womanhood imposed on them by patriarchal cultures, women were confronted by a new challenge as they journeyed from Cairo to Beijing. This challenge was to shift from the reactive mindset of those who are subjected to systematic discrimination and made to feel powerless, to the proactive mindset of those who have a strong sense of personal identity, autonomy, and efficacy as makers of their own lives. I hoped, as I went to the Fourth World Conference on Women in Beijing (1995), with thousands of others, that women in general, and Muslim women in particular, would be able to build on the hard-won gains of the Cairo conference and begin to speak of themselves as full and autonomous human beings who have not only a body but also a mind and a spirit.

Unfortunately, however, what happened at Beijing was a reversal, almost a betrayal, of the promise that had been seen and felt at Cairo. Instead of engaging in a critical dialogue on the existential situation of the majority of Muslim women in the world who have three characteristics—they are poor, illiterate, and live in a village—the spokespersons of the most visible groups of Muslims at the NGO (nongovernmental organization) Forum in Beijing denied that Muslim women had any serious problems that needed to be addressed. Instead of confronting the indisputable fact that Muslim culture, like other patriarchal cultures, is pervaded by anti-women biases that have a negative impact on every aspect of women's lives, these spokespersons not only defended but glorified whatever goes under the name of Islam in traditional Muslim societies. As the Beijing conference drew to a close, it seemed that the hope of a paradigm shift from reactive to proactive thinking that had come to birth at Cairo was likely—like female children in pre-Islamic Arabia—to be buried alive.

For "liberal" Muslims there were important lessons to be learned from the experiences at Cairo and Beijing. Paramount among them was the need to understand the role of religion and culture in Muslim societies and communities and the discrepancy between the norms or ideals of Islam's primary sources and Muslim practice with regard to women and women-related issues. A deep analysis of Muslim history, particularly of modern times, and the political, economic, social, and psychological factors that have had a formative influence on Muslim consciousness was also required.

That "liberal" Muslims in general had not done the hard work required to make a compelling case in support of a "liberal" or "progressive" approach to understanding Islam was apparent at Beijing. Perhaps like many other "liberals," they had assumed that what they had to say was inherently so reasonable or rational that it could be regarded as self-evident, requiring no corroborative data. But what the conferences at Cairo and Beijing have demonstrated is that the greatest impact is made by those who have done their homework best.

If liberal Muslim women are capable of insensitivity to the painful contradictions in their own movements, it is hardly surprising that Western feminists can be guilty of an incomplete understanding of the reality of Muslim women. The aversion to religion, especially Islam, that pervades the U.S. women's movement undercuts their genuine efforts to empower Muslim women. They hope that after "liberation" from the Taliban, Afghan women will throw off their *burqas,* cast off their Islamic and Afghan identities, and become "secular."

Every one of the Afghan women I have known in the United States, Pakistan, and elsewhere has made it clear to me that for them the reconstruction and reform of Afghan society does not mean an abandonment of Islam or Afghan cultural heritage. Afghan women are going to need a lot of support from women all over the world in rebuilding their lives and their country. The women's movement in the United States, which is diverse in so many ways, being multireligious, multicultural, and multiethnic, is certainly called upon to play a major role in providing this support. Yet the support that is offered to Afghan women, whether it is political, economic, medical, social, or any other, must be given without the expectation or the demand that Afghan women will follow a donor-driven agenda, especially one that is rooted in aversion to Islam and Afghan culture.

From my perspective, one reason why religious extremism became so vocal and visible in the last three decades was that Western donors poured a huge amount of support into "antireligious" organizations, which insist that human rights and Islam are incompatible. To many

Muslims the Qur'an is the Magna Carta of human rights. A large part of the Qur'an's concern is to free human beings from the bondage of traditionalism, authoritarianism (religious, political, economic, or any other), tribalism, racism, sexism, slavery, or anything else that prohibits or inhibits human beings from actualizing the Qur'anic vision of human destiny embodied in the classic proclamation: "Toward Allah is thy limit."

After the Iranian Revolution in 1979, when both superpowers reacted in panic to what they saw as the impending threat of the spread of Islamic "fundamentalism," many Western donor agencies began to support a number of "secular" human rights and women's organizations in Muslim countries. While in its classic sense, the word "secular" refers to what is outside of ecclesiastical authority, or "nonreligious," in Muslim societies it is generally understood as "antireligious" or "anti-Islamic." One kind of extremism feeds another kind of extremism, and the more the "antireligious" extremists in Pakistan expressed their aversion or antagonism to Islam, the more the "religious extremists" raised the slogan of "Islam in danger" to rally people behind them.

In my view, anyone who says that human rights and Islam are incompatible has not read the Qur'an, which strongly affirms fundamental human rights. The fact that in recent decades, particularly since the Iranian Revolution, a number of Muslim countries have turned to normative Islamic teachings in their effort to establish a framework for their temporal as well as spiritual development does not mean that these countries cannot have a just social system. On the contrary, any paradigm of human rights or self-actualization that is constructed outside of the belief system of the people living in a particular society is likely to be regarded as irrelevant. In societies that are overwhelmingly and profoundly Muslim, as is the case in Afghanistan and Pakistan, programs of action that violate or disregard what is of central value and meaning to the masses of people are doomed to failure.

Since the modern notion of human rights originated in a Western, secular context, Muslims in general, but Muslim women in particular, find themselves in a quandary when they initiate, or participate in, a discussion on human rights, whether in the West or in Muslim societies. Based on their life experience, most Muslim women who become human rights advocates or activists feel strongly that virtually all Muslim societies discriminate against women from cradle to grave. This leads many of them to become deeply alienated from Muslim culture in a number of ways. This bitter sense of alienation oftentimes leads to anger and bitterness toward the patriarchal systems of thought and social structures that dominate most Muslim societies.

Muslim women often find much support and sympathy in the West so long as they are seen as rebels and deviants within the world of Islam. But many of them begin to realize, sooner or later, that while they have serious difficulties with Muslim culture, they are also not able, for many reasons, to identify with Western, secular culture.

Much attention has been focused in Western media and literature on the sorry plight of Muslim women who are "poor and oppressed" in visible or tangible ways. Since the rise of the Taliban, and especially since September 11, the U.S. women's movement, in an urgent desire to help Afghan women, have lent their support to the most radical and Westernized element of the Afghan women's movement. Hardly any notice has been taken, however, of the vast majority of Afghan women who are struggling to maintain their religious identity and personal autonomy in the face of the intransigence of Muslim culture on the one hand, and the imperialism of Western, secular culture on the other hand.

At the Beijing conference, the slogan that acquired global currency was "Sisterhood is Global." If sisterhood is indeed global, then I hope that those groups in the U.S. women's movement that have a hegemonic mindset and may seek to pressure Afghan women, especially those whom they have patronized in difficult times, will do something extraordinary. I hope they will be able to transcend their personal agendas and support their Afghan sisters in attaining goals that they have set for themselves within a framework of their own choosing.

UNITED NATIONS AND AFGHANISTAN

ANGELA E. V. KING

THE WOMEN OF AFGHANISTAN have been a great concern in my work, especially since 1997, when I led a United Nations (UN) Interagency Gender Mission to Afghanistan at the request of the secretary-general and the Executive Committee for Humanitarian Affairs.[1] The mission's goal was to assess the situation of women in Afghanistan, to propose guidelines for the integration of gender concerns in all UN assistance programs, and to recommend monitoring and accountability mechanisms. The assistance community at the time, and in the following years, faced the challenge of finding a balance between taking a principled approach to the equal participation of women and men, on one hand, and the great need for immediate life-sustaining assistance despite political obstacles, on the other. The difficulties of addressing the humanitarian crisis were heightened by the ongoing armed conflict and by an extremist political regime in the form of the Taliban, which denied women their basic rights to healthcare, education, employment, and a life free of violence. Since my introduction to Afghanistan and my meetings with Afghan women, who despite the most difficult circumstances continued to support their families and communities within Afghanistan and in refugee camps in neighboring countries, I continued to follow the developments in the country. And I attempted to influence, within my capacity, the shaping of UN policies on Afghanistan.

The United Nations and its family of organizations have a long history of support and cooperation in Afghanistan. Over the years of conflict and more seriously since the takeover of Kabul in 1996 by the Taliban, the secretary-general and the Security Council repeatedly addressed the problems besetting that country. The Council's interest in gender issues and the impact of conflict on women and men increased steadily, with debates in 1997 and one specifically on gender issues in April 2000. The General Assembly, the Economic and Social Council, and the Commissions on the Status of Women and Human Rights, as well as the special rapporteur on the situation of human rights in Afghanistan and the special rapporteur on violence against women, its causes, and consequences, have also paid special attention to the situation of women in Afghanistan.

In the fall of 2001, the conflict in Afghanistan took a dramatic turn with the military intervention of the United States and its allies. Despite many years of concern over and advocacy for Afghan women, it took a major tragedy to put Afghanistan at the center of world attention and highlight the situation of Afghan women.

The UN system reacted through a fast-moving strategic framework in three areas: the political arena, humanitarian assistance, and reconstruction and development. The secretary-general reappointed Lakhdar Brahimi as his special representative to oversee the United Nation's efforts to establish an interim administration in Afghanistan and develop plans for the rehabilitation and reconstruction of the country. At UN headquarters, the first Integrated Mission Task Force (IMTF) was established to advise the special representative as well as to coordinate and prepare strategies based on input from the executive committees and the field, through the resident/humanitarian coordinator. The IMTF included a gender specialist from the Division on the Advancement of Women (DAW). Three Executive Committees, reporting to the secretary-general on Peace and Security, Humanitarian Affairs, and the United Nations Development Group (UNDG), each comprising agencies engaged in related work, met regularly and drew up strategic recovery plans on the political process, humanitarian assistance, and re-construction of the country, including gender perspectives. In addition, the UNDG and the Executive Committee on Humanitarian Affairs formed a subgroup on gender in Afghanistan. This subgroup was created to ensure the inclusion of a gender perspective in the peace negotiations and in the needs assessment for the International Conference on Reconstruction Assistance to Afghanistan, which was held in Tokyo in January 2002. In addition, this subgroup was to monitor the inclusion of women in the reconstruction process.

The United Nations hosted talks on a transitional government for Afghanistan in Bonn from November 27 to December 5, 2001 under the leadership of Lakhdar Brahimi. Four Afghan groups participated, representing respectively the Rome process, which was linked to the former king; the United Front (also known as the Northern Alliance); the Cyprus Group; and the Peshawar Group.[2] The United Nations had strongly encouraged all political groups to include women in their delegations, and Afghan women's organizations were asked to contact the four groups to participate in the talks. However, it was not the role of the United Nations to select representatives. Afghans had to take ownership by selecting their own participants. Two women, Sima Wali and Rona Mansuri, participated as full delegates of the Rome process; Amena Afzali as a full delegate of the United Front; Seddiqa Balkhi as advisor to the Cyprus Group; and Fatana Gilani as advisor to the Peshawar Group.

The Agreement on Provisional Arrangements in Afghanistan, pending the reestablishment of permanent government institutions (hereafter called the agreement), was signed in Bonn on December 5, 2001. It noted that these interim arrangements were intended "as a first step toward the establishment of a broad-based, gender-sensitive, multi-ethnic and fully representative government."[3] The Interim Authority consists of an interim administration, a Special Independent Commission for the convening of the Emergency *Loya Jirga* (traditional assembly of elders), and a Supreme Court of Afghanistan.

The agreement set up a twenty-nine-member cabinet for six months, which is composed "with due regard to the ethnic, geographic and religious composition of Afghanistan and to the importance of the participation of women."[4] The Interim Authority, headed by Hamid Karzai, took office on December 22, 2001, in Kabul. The agreement provided that two ministries would be run by women: the Ministry of Women's Affairs, which had never before existed, and the Ministry of Public Health. The Ministry of Women's Affairs is headed by Sima Samar, a physician and founder of the Shuhada Organization, a network of clinics, hospitals, and schools in Pakistan and central Afghanistan. She is also one of five vice presidents of the Interim Authority. Suhaila Seddiqi, the minister of public health, is a former army general and a surgeon who continued to practice in Kabul throughout the Taliban regime.

In January 2002, the Special Independent Commission to Convene the Emergency *Loya Jirga* was set up, with three women among its twenty-one members: Mahbooba Hoquqmal, who is also a vice chair; Humaira Nematy; and Soraya Parlika. The Special Independent Commission has the responsibility of ensuring that "due attention is paid to the representation in the Emergency *Loya Jirga* of a significant number of women."[5]

The representation of women in the Interim Authority and the Special Commission are positive developments, but the Ministry of Women's Affairs was not given an office, a staff, or funding for months. Assistance needs to be provided there as well as to all line ministries, to develop the capacity to integrate a gender perspective into their programs. Furthermore, women need to participate in all specialized commissions, such as those on human rights, civil service, and the judiciary; and the mandates of those commissions must address gender issues.

To accelerate the relief and reconstruction processes, an International Conference on Reconstruction Assistance to Afghanistan took place in Tokyo on January 21 and 22, 2002, to which the World Bank, the Asian Development Bank, and the UN Development Programme submitted a joint needs assessment for recovery and reconstruction. According to preliminary estimates, the reconstruction of Afghanistan would require about $15 billion over the next ten years. The Tokyo meeting, which highlighted education for girls as one of the key priorities for the reconstruction of the country, concluded with pledges and contributions of over $4.5 billion U.S. for the next few years, including $1.8 billion for 2002.

Notwithstanding the lack of systematic data collection and time and security constraints, the needs assessment provided helpful information and projections. It is expected that more consultations will be held with Afghan stakeholders to confirm priorities and medium- and long-term funding requirements and to conduct a thorough needs assessment, including a gender dimension in all sectors and the collection of data disaggregated by sex and age. This assessment will also require clear indicators to measure actual changes in the status of women and girls.

AFGHAN WOMEN'S VOICES

In response to requests from Afghan women and in collaboration with the Office of the Special Adviser on Gender Issues and Advancement of Women and the United Nations Development Fund for Women (UNIFEM), a number of nongovernmental organizations (NGOs) convened the Afghan Women's Summit for Democracy in Brussels on December 4 and 5, 2001.[6] Approximately forty Afghan women leaders from different ethnic, linguistic, and religious backgrounds participated, including three who had also attended the UN negotiations in Bonn. In a message to the summit, the secretary-general assured the participants of the full and unstinting support of the United Nations and emphasized that there cannot be peace and recovery in Afghanistan without the restoration of the rights of women.[7]

The summit concluded with the adoption of the Brussels Proclamation,[8] which included concrete demands for the recovery of Afghan society in the areas of education, media, culture, health, human rights, the constitution, refugees, and internally displaced women. The proclamation's demands included the following:

- The right of women to vote and to receive equal pay
- The right to equal access to healthcare, education, and employment
- An emergency plan for reopening schools by March 2002 for both girls and boys
- The training of teachers
- The inclusion of Afghan women lawyers in the development of a new constitution
- The rebuilding of hospitals
- Provision for healthcare, including psychological counseling
- The inclusion of women in the Emergency *Loya Jirga*
- The protection of women from forced underage marriages and sexual harassment.

Participants of the summit met with members of the European Parliament, members of the U.S. Congress, members of the Security Council in an Arria Formula meeting,[9] and women ambassadors to the United Nations. In their talks, the Afghan women called for measures to increase security in Afghanistan and facilitate the disarmament of all warring factions. The secretary-general met with them to hear their priorities and concerns.

In cooperation with the government of Belgium, UNIFEM organized a roundtable in Brussels on December 10 and 11, 2001, entitled "Building Women's Leadership in Afghanistan." The roundtable, which brought together Afghan women and UN agencies, the World Bank, and donors, issued an action plan calling for mechanisms to support the role and leadership of women in shaping the future of their country.[10]

Numerous other panels and conferences have been organized by and with Afghan women's organizations inside and outside Afghanistan to ensure that the experiences and needs of Afghan women receive attention in all efforts directed at post-Taliban Afghanistan. Schools for girls have been reopened and women are seeking to return to their former professions. The first radio and television broadcast in Kabul featured a woman speaker.

Unfortunately, a less positive picture has also appeared. It became apparent that women's rights and freedoms could not be taken for granted when the then-minister of the interior of the United Front informed the organizers of the new Union of Women in Afghanistan that their planned marches through Kabul on November 20 and 27, 2001, could not proceed because of security concerns.[11]

There were also reports that some women left behind by retreating Taliban had become victims of anti-Taliban reactions and that other women had been abducted from the Kabul area by fleeing Taliban. The fate of these women remains unclear. According to press reports, the minister of justice of the Interim Authority promised to investigate cases of the kidnapping of women, but he indicated that this would be difficult as some women were forced to marry Taliban officers or were trafficked outside of Afghanistan.[12] According to the minister, the Taliban had regularly sold women as sex slaves to fund its regime.

CHALLENGES FOR THE FUTURE

For the first time in many years, there is a groundswell of concern from parliaments to first ladies, from media stars to nongovernmental organizations (NGOs). All are calling for the full recognition of Afghan women's rights and freedoms in a society where severe and institutionalized gender discrimination and gender-based violence prevailed in the past.

The fall of the Taliban and the establishment of the Interim Authority have clearly created new opportunities for Afghan women, but most obstacles to women's full enjoyment of their rights continue to exist. Estimates indicate that every year 15,000 women die from pregnancy-related causes; 25 percent of children die before they reach five years of age; 4 percent of the population is disabled, many from mines. According to a recent report by Physicians for Human Rights, 70 percent of women who lived in Taliban-controlled areas meet the criteria for depression. Only 12 percent of the population has access to adequate sanitation.[13] Due to twenty-three years of armed conflict and three years of severe drought, the overall level of development in Afghanistan is very low. Prior to 1979, Afghanistan was one of the poorest countries of the world with high maternal and child mortality rates and very low literacy rates for women.

Reference is often made to women having constituted 70 percent of teachers, 50 percent of civil servants, and 40 percent of medical doctors in Kabul before the civil war. However, it should be noted that in the 1980s, the female adult literacy rate was only 8 percent.[14] While women had undoubtedly made much progress in different professional fields, these advances were limited to urban areas, particularly Kabul. The fact that the overall literacy rate was so low indicated that future interventions must do more than address a need for girls and women to catch up on educational opportunities missed during the Taliban regime. It is necessary to develop an educational system that will reach all children throughout the country. Along the same lines, access to basic health services for all women and men in Afghanistan needs to be created, not just repaired.

Although much attention was drawn to the imposition of the *burqa* (the full-length veil covering the entire body, also known as *chadari*) on Afghan women as the perhaps most visible form of discrimination, Afghan women themselves consider other forms of discrimination, such as the ban on employment and education, of greater significance. It is important to note that the violations of women's rights did not start with the Taliban regime. Women had been consistently discriminated against and marginalized before the Taliban came to power in a system of traditional kinship where gender relations within the family unit, as well as within the local community, were dominated by males.

Efforts by the international assistance community, the United Nations, NGOs, and donors to advance the status of women should therefore be based on a thorough understanding of the local culture and customs within this Muslim society and on the priorities of Afghan women as they themselves define them.

The treatment of women during the civil war and particularly during the Taliban regime tends to perpetuate a perception of women as victims. Although women were traditionally assigned roles within the family, in reality, they assumed greater economic and social responsibilities during the years of conflict. This development occurred largely because of the absence of men, the displacement of women from their homes, and changes in their social networks as a result of that displacement. There is a gap, therefore, between the actual situation of women as lived, on one hand, and generally accepted norms based on tradition and custom, on the other. Future interventions by the assistance community must reckon with this gap by working with both women and men on issues related to gender equality.[15]

It is important to see women as primary stakeholders and agents of change. They must play a crucial role in identifying their needs and priorities in all sectors of society. The United Nations and the international assistance community will have to ensure a consistent and principled approach to gender mainstreaming by giving Afghan women ownership of the process. Furthermore, it will be crucial for the success of interventions on behalf of women to ensure that the assistance community leads by example in its own operations.

A safe environment, free from violence, discrimination, and abuse for all Afghans, is a precondition for a viable and sustainable recovery and reconstruction process. The civil war and the militarization of society have fostered a culture of violence against women and girls that is likely to continue to affect them during peacetime. The change in power and current instability may lead to increased violence against women in an atmosphere of impunity with regard to that violence. Special measures need to be taken to protect women and girls from forced and underage marriages and all other forms of violence. In this context, studying the existing legal system with regard to family law, divorce, property rights, and inheritance rights is a high priority.

In summary, special attention *must* be directed at the promotion and protection of the human rights of women and girls in Afghanistan, including the right to nondiscrimination with regard to sex, age, religion, ethnicity, disability, and political affiliation. Women's effective participation in civil, cultural, economic, political, and social life should be promoted and protected throughout the country. These areas encompass the right to:

- Life
- Work
- Education
- Security of person
- Freedom of movement and association
- Freedom of opinion and expression
- Equal access to facilities necessary to protect their right to the highest attainable physical and mental health.

The international community will have to ensure that support for Afghan women moves beyond lip service to the recognition that Afghan women are entitled to be full partners in all decision-making processes related to governance, humanitarian efforts, and reconstruction of their country.

NOTES

1. The mission consisted of representatives of the Economic and Social Commission for Western Asia (ESCWA), United Nations Population Fund (UNFPA), United Nations Development Programme (UNDP), United Nations Children's Fund (UNICEF), World Food Program (WFP), and World Health Organization (WHO).
2. From the late 1990s, Afghans in exile began to organize politically in response to the Taliban regime. Four initiatives emerged: the Rome process led by King Zahir Shah, the Cyprus process, the Bonn process, and the Pe-

shawar process. Each of these bodies had delegates at the Bonn meetings of November 2001, which led to the formation of the interim government. (Editor)

3. For the agreement, go to: www.uno.de/frieden/Afghanistan/talks/agreement.htm
4. Ibid., para. III.A.3.
5. Ibid., para.IV.2.
6. The organization consisted of the European Women's Lobby, Equality Now, V-Day, Center for Strategic Initiatives of Women, and Feminist Majority Foundation.
7. "True Afghan Peace Not Possible Without Restoration of Women's Rights": www.un.org/News/Press/docs/2001/sgsm8066.doc.htm
8. See: www.un.org/womenwatch/afghanistan/documents/Brussels_proclamation.pdf
9. An informal meeting between Security Council members and non-members, including individual experts and representatives of NGOs.
10. "Brussels Action Plan," Afghan Women's Participation in the Reconstruction of Afghanistan": www.unifem.undp.org/pr_afghanistan.html
11. Chris Foley, "Northern Alliance Bans Women's Freedom March in Kabul," Agence France Presse (AFP), November 27, 2001.
12. Kevin Sullivan, "Kabul's Lost Women. Many Abducted by Taliban Still Missing," *Washington Post,* December 19, 2001.
13. Physicians for Human Rights, *Women's Health and Human Rights in Afghanistan, A Population-Based Assessment* (Boston and Washington D.C.) 2001. See www.phrusa.org/campaigns/afghanistan/afghan_report.html.
14. UNICEF, *The State of the World's Children,* 1989.
15. UNICEF, "Future Directions in Women's Role and Status in Afghanistan: An Afghan Perspective," November 2001.

WOMEN ARE OPENING DOORS

SECURITY COUNCIL RESOLUTION 1325 IN AFGHANISTAN

FELICITY HILL AND MIKELE ABOITIZ

AFTER SEPTEMBER 11, 2001, the world became aware of the suffering of women in Afghanistan. Women's nongovernmental organizations (NGOs) around the world had been trying to raise awareness for years, but only after September 11 did these women appear so prominently in the *New York Times,* the *Washington Post,* and on CNN and similar high-profile news media. Only then did women appear on the radar screen of international policy makers. International media attention focused on the Taliban's war on Afghan women, with less attention given to the need for women to be present at the peace table.

As the U.S.-led war in Afghanistan developed, women's organizations around the world saw an opportunity to turn a terrible situation into a positive outcome. It was not enough that the Taliban were pushed out of Afghanistan; it was not enough that the United States and the international community spoke about women's issues. It was time to let women speak for themselves and decide their future.

WILPF AND THE NGO WORKING GROUP ON WOMEN, PEACE, AND SECURITY

At the Women's International League for Peace and Freedom (WILPF),[1] the process of empowering women to find peace started a long time ago. WILPF is an old and well-established organization, dating back to 1915, when its founders and leaders outlined a new and compassionate concept of human security. That year some 1,300 women from Europe and North America gathered in The Hague, the Netherlands. These women originated both from countries at war with each other and from countries that were neutral. All came together in a congress of women to protest the killing and destruction wrought by the war raging in Europe. They envisioned a security that does not rest on military strength but rather lies in equitable and sustainable economic and social development.

These 1,300 women issued 20 resolutions; some were of immediate importance, while others aimed at reducing conflict and preventing war by establishing the foundation for a permanent peace among the world's nations. Neutral governments were called on to press warring nations to stop fighting and settle their differences by negotiations that would be held within the borders of neutral countries. Grievances and remedies would be voiced and met with impartiality.

This vision translates into an equal distribution of resources to meet the basic needs of all people and guarantees full and equal participation of men and women in all levels of society, including decisionmaking. The women organized "envoys" to carry these resolutions to both neutral and belligerent states in Europe and to the president of the United States. Jane Addams, having been elected president of the congress and of the International Women's Committee (the beginning of WILPF), met with President Woodrow Wilson, who, according to government records, said that the congress's resolutions were by far the best formations for peace that had been put forward to date.[2] Again, according to the records, Wilson "borrowed" some of their ideas for his own peace proposals. In total, the congress had small delegations that visited fourteen countries during May and June of 1915. WILPF was founded as an international organization to work globally. Two of WILPF's original founders, Jane Addams and Emily Greene Balch, received the Nobel Peace Prize, in 1931 and 1946, respectively, for their peace efforts and international views and work.

Women's voices are needed not only at the negotiating tables but also in the larger political institutions that generate and dictate security policy. The utter failure of current conceptions of security, largely defined by men, suggests the need for new approaches by new people. The full and equal participation of women at all levels of national and international life would undoubtedly contribute to addressing the current human security vacuum. Women are still suffering disproportionately in situations of armed conflict, but as more women participate in decision making and negotiating peace and security issues, the hope is that armed conflict will no longer be a tolerable solution and that preparation for armed conflict will not be confused with security.

With this concept in mind, WILPF has organized rallies, lobbied politicians, and pushed members of the United Nations (UN) to find solutions to inequalities as a means of solving all armed conflicts. In 2001 WILPF joined Amnesty International, the Hague Appeal for Peace, International Alert, International Peace Research Association, and the Women's Commission for Refugee Women and Children, and created the NGO Working Group on Women and International Peace and Security. This working group seized a window of opportunity and pushed for a thematic debate in the United Nations Security Council after Ambassador Anwarul Karim Chowdhury of Bangladesh, president of the Security Council, made a ground-breaking statement on March 8, 2000, linking equality, development, peace, and the need for women's urgent involvement in these matters. The combination of contributions from the Namibian presidency of the Security Council, the NGO Working Group, the Division for the Advancement of Women (DAW), and the United Nations Development Fund for

Women (UNIFEM) helped to identify and bring the experiences and expertise of civil society into the sacred and once-exclusive realm of the Security Council.

Besides creating a list of experts and NGOs that would speak to the issues in the Security Council, members of the working group lobbied and debated with every Security Council member. Furthermore, they compiled packets of relevant documents with summaries that they hand-delivered to all Security Council members and undertook media strategy to maximize attention on this issue. Synergy among NGOs, UN departments, and governments brought together the strengths of each segment and ensured success. Representatives of WILPF expressed hope and relief that issues so long ignored were at last being registered at the highest levels.

SECURITY COUNCIL RESOLUTION 1325

It was a profoundly moving and historic moment when women at last filled the public gallery of the Security Council on October 24, 2000, applauding and cheering. After fifty-five years of efforts on the part of the United Nations to end the scourge of war, women's perspectives on war and peace had finally been acknowledged in the Security Council. Women from Sierra Leone, Guatemala, Somalia, Tanzania, and international NGOs had spoken to members of the Security Council in an Arria Formula meeting[3] the previous day. Arria Formula meetings offer an opportunity for NGO experts to brief the ambassadors on specific topics. These meetings focused on the suffering of women in war, their undervalued and underutilized work to prevent conflict and build peace, and the leadership they demonstrate in rebuilding wartorn societies.

As a result, on October 31, 2000, Security Council members unanimously passed Resolution 1325, which calls for:

- The participation of women in decision-making and peace processes

- Gender perspectives and training in peacekeeping
- The protection of women
- Gender mainstreaming in UN reporting systems and programmatic implementation mechanisms.

Resolution 1325 provides a tool for women because it requires gender sensitivity in all UN missions including peacekeeping, women's equal participation at all negotiating tables, and the protection of women and girls during armed conflict. The last paragraph of this resolution notes that the Security Council "decides to remain actively seized of the matter." This resolution provides an important tool in shifting the UN system from words to action.

SC 1325 IN ACTION: AFGHANISTAN

On the surface, Resolution 1325 may seem like empty words, but for women's groups involved in peace building in conflict zones worldwide, it is a historic statement with significant implications that can be quoted and used in related contexts. Moreover, as a Security Council resolution, it is binding international law that for the first time officially endorses the inclusion of civil society groups, notably women, in peace processes and in the implementation of peace agreements. Women finally have a tool they can use to become part of the planning for the future of their country. Afghan and non-Afghan women have used this resolution to demand that Mr. Lakhdar Brahimi, the secretary-general's special representative for Afghanistan, meet with Afghan women and hear their voices. He took the first step by meeting with five Afghan women immediately after he was appointed.

The United Nations strongly supported the inclusion of women at the Bonn meetings in December 2001. Because of the prioritization of this issue, a few women did participate in the Bonn negotiations. However, the presence of a mere three women as delegates and two as advisors is not enough. Women's involvement in these matters cannot be restricted to a small number of token individuals who are supposed to represent all women. Three people cannot represent so many others, especially when the population they represent is as disparate as Afghan women.

However, acknowledging that there is much room for improvement does not by any means diminish the importance and historic achievement of the participation of women at Bonn. Considering that women are usually absent at high decision-making levels and virtually invisible from negotiations on cease-fires, peace agreements, and postconflict reconstruction, women activists for peace did feel some sense of accomplishment in the participation of five women at the Bonn negotiations. Years of activism, raising awareness, and conferences organized by women in New York, Berlin, and all over the world played a major part in that achievement. We regard it as a turning point and an important benchmark along the road to full and equal participation for women in all aspects and at all levels of governance.

Women rarely participate in negotiating cease-fires and drafting treaties because they do not occupy leadership positions in governments or other armed groups. Women are not leading warring parties. Rather, women constitute the majority of those executed, enslaved, impoverished, and damaged. Ultimately, however, women must be involved in the peace process not only because they suffer disproportionately, or because they have previously been excluded, but because their contribution to the world is invaluable.

If the importance of the resolution is recognized, it will have profound implications for change. It has the potential to be an effective tool in the hands of the United Nations, NGOs, and governments. In order to ensure collaboration and coordination, Secretary-General Kofi Annan established a task force on women, peace, and security, composed of representatives from fifteen UN entities. This task force is developing an action plan on the implementation of the resolution and will produce a comprehensive report on the role of the United Nations within the year.

UNIFEM also appointed two independent experts who will produce a report with recommendations to the United Nations, governments, and NGOs. The Office of the Coordination of Humanitarian Affairs (OCHA) launched its fund-raising appeal immediately after the resolution was passed to benefit women in conflict zones. The Department for Disarmament Affairs produced a series of briefing papers showing the connections between gender and the full range of disarmament issues, land mines, small arms, weapons of mass destruction, and the peace movement. These developments are only a few examples of the shifting climate within the United Nations.

A LOOK INTO THE FUTURE

Since the passage of this momentous Resolution, reports on UN peacekeeping operations, such as those on Afghanistan (S/2000/1106), the Democratic Republic of Congo (S/2001/128), Western Sahara (S/2001/148), and other countries, have included material on gender and the situation of women in their countries. The gender unit in East Timor is outstanding in the kinds of reports and information it has produced for the Department of Peace Keeping Operations and the Security Council. It has shown concretely that the efforts of the United Nations on gender, while difficult to establish at first, have enhanced the effectiveness and the sense of integrity of the United Nations in the field. The training that has taken place through the Gender Unit in East Timor will enable women to occupy key positions in the new government. The technical assistance and guidance given to NGOs trying to navigate the sometimes intimidating UN system should not be underestimated.

Men still disproportionately dominate all of the formal governing bodies of peace and security. Let's face it—they have totally and utterly failed in their efforts. Wars continue to rage everywhere. The fragility of the most militarily powerful nation on earth is exposed. And the result of militarizing countries—arming, training, and paying thugs—turns out to be the formula for antisecurity.

To pressure their governments to take action, women's groups must be made aware of treaties and laws that have been agreed on by their governments to address gender concerns. Nongovernmental organizations can support and sustain women's efforts using the tools provided in Resolution 1325 by:

- Pressing governments to increase the numbers of senior women in the United Nations
- Contributing women's names to rosters for these positions
- Pressing for greater involvement of national and international negotiators in conflict zones and monitoring their actions
- Ensuring that local civil society groups are integrated into all levels and aspects of conflict prevention, resolution, and management
- Lobbying governments to contribute funds for gender training of peacekeepers
- Ensuring gender training in armies
- Monitoring and documenting the actions of peacekeepers vis-à-vis women and girls
- Monitoring and lobbying for increased civil society involvement in the design and implementation of humanitarian assistance programs in refugee camps
- Collecting gender-sensitive data and testimonies to provide greater accuracy and understanding of the needs of refugees and internally displaced persons
- Monitoring the implementation of Resolution 1325 at national and international levels
- Lobbying for greater consultation with UN agencies in follow-up processes and reports.

A WILPF project in the works will help women monitor progress and share news, campaigning tools, and contact details. Our new website (www.peacewomen.org) aims to pull together the efforts of women working for peace in conflict zones. We wish to make it impossible for the world, especially the United Nations, to ignore the peacebuilding work of women. We exist to support women in their efforts to attain peace and justice, abolish oppression, and to challenge colonialism, discrimination, aggression, occupation, and foreign domination.

One section of the site gathers a comprehensive database of women's organizations in every country to facilitate networking and resourcing. Another section provides a collection of resources, including annotated bibliographies of books, articles, NGO reports, and tools for organizational building that feed critical thinking on sexism and militarism and enable women's groups to proceed in their work better informed. The third part translates the UN resolution into understandable language, focusing on war, peace, and security, and highlighting UN efforts that pertain particularly to women affected by war. The final section features campaigns and news of women who are working for peace and justice around the world.

The words of Security Council Resolution 1325 have translated into action and must continue to do so. The people who comprise the United Nations must ensure that women are included at every level of peace and security, from local communities to international criminal tribunals for countries coming out of conflict.

The doors were open just wide enough for women to squeeze into the peace negotiations in Afghanistan. They came with the knowledge that war is a gendered activity. Now, concerned women and men must use the words of Resolution 1325 to force the doors permanently open, to enter *all* rooms where peace agreements are negotiated and where peacekeeping operations are planned. Afghanistan must be the testing ground for the implementation of Resolution 1325.

NOTES

1. WILPF has offices in New York City and Geneva.
2. Gertrude Bussey and Margaret Tims, *Pioneers for Peace, Women's International League for Peace and Freedom: 1915–1917* (Oxford, U.K.: Alden Press, 1980), p. 21.

3. Informal, off-the-record exchanges between security council members and NGOs, often used to provide expert testimony on specific issues, particularly humanitarian concerns.

I HOPE THIS LETTER WILL REACH YOU

Irena Lieberman

I hope this letter will reach you. I am a mother, and I have suffered very badly. . . . One of the Talibs asked us to agree to the marriage of our young daughter or else be killed. We refused and one of the Talibs stabbed me with a knife when I tried to protect her. . . . They abducted my daughter by force and used her for sex-slavery under the name of marriage. When we insisted on searching for our daughter, they threatened to kill us all if we remained in Kabul . . . we felt that our lives were in danger, and we could not stay any longer in Afghanistan and we had to escape. My daughter was abandoned after one year on the street in Kabul. Here in Peshawar we are not feeling safe either due to the Taliban supporters' threats. Please help me join my family in the U.S. Please help us; we cannot afford the fear and pain any more.

—an Afghan woman writing to the Tahirih Justice Center

WORKING ON BEHALF OF AFGHAN WOMEN has truly been an honor and inspiration to me since I began practicing law in 1998. I chose this work first and foremost as a woman outraged by the epidemic of misogyny that still persists across the globe. My upbringing as the daughter of a refugee who herself fled ethnic and religious persecution also informed my desire to assist those facing unspeakable human rights abuses in their pursuit of justice.

The Tahirih Justice Center, a nonprofit, pro bono legal services organization in Falls Church, Virginia, has been working to protect women and girls from gender-based persecution, such as domestic violence, honor crimes, female genital mutilation, rape, sex slavery, trafficking, and other abuses since its inception in the fall of 1997. In April 1999 the center launched its Afghan Refugee Women Advocacy Project (the project) in response to the growing number of requests for help that we began receiving from women fleeing Afghanistan into neighboring countries such as Pakistan, Iran, India, and Russia.[1] While intense in their passion for their country, like the woman quoted in the epigraph, the women who called for help had reached a crossroads where they could no longer endure the imminent threats to their lives that remaining in Afghanistan or Pakistan posed. In each woman's life story, she and/or her daughters were fleeing abuses such as torture, imprisonment, rape, domestic violence, forced marriage, stoning, or numerous other atrocities—all for the simple reason that they were women.

The Afghan refugee women who continue to call me are in search of resettlement in the United States and other countries where they will be safe from persecution. Resettlement may be a short-term, Band-Aid solution that does not address the larger goals of rebuilding a safe and peaceful Afghanistan, but it is not intended to fulfill such broader goals. Instead, the purpose of the project is to serve the acute, emergent needs of my clients as they express them to me. Typically, my clients seek resettlement to ensure their basic survival. For most, resettlement in the United States means not having to live in hiding, not living in constant fear, and having access to medical care for themselves and their children.

I represent women who have already made their way to the United States in political asylum cases so that they will be allowed to remain here and live in safety. For some clients who were human rights workers in Afghanistan, remaining in the United States enables them to continue their life's work on behalf of other women. I also advocate for women outside the United States so that they will be allowed entry into the country as refugees. Although the center's immediate goal is to reach out to individual women, we also aim to help bring about systemic change through our direct services. We hope to educate asylum adjudicators and to promote a more accessible resettlement application process for our clients.

Through litigating cases on behalf of women and girls, I have learned that they face challenges in their pursuit of legal protections over and above those faced by asylum-seekers who are not fleeing persecution on account of their gender. In fact, the unique challenges most of my female clients face are a direct result of their gender. Regardless of a woman's country of origin, there may be certain cultural protocols that are in direct conflict with what is required for an applicant to present a strong asylum or refugee resettlement case.

ANY WOMAN'S JOURNEY: SEEKING REFUGE FROM GENDER-BASED VIOLENCE

Consider the story of a woman whom I shall call "Maya" as an illustration of some of the obstacles women face as they navigate the legal system. Maya has been raped. In her culture, as in many others, the woman is blamed when she is raped. People in her community will believe she provoked it—*invited* it—and she will be punished accordingly. She may be punished under the law of her country—for example, she may be thrown in jail. She may also be punished by nongovernment agents such as her husband, her family, or strangers. She may be ostracized, taunted, harassed, shunned, beaten, mutilated—all because of the actions of another. As a result, Maya does not dare report the rape to the police. The police may disbelieve her, tell her husband, or have her imprisoned. They may laugh at her, tell her she deserved it, or rape her themselves. A police officer may have been her rapist, and he knows where she lives and when she is home.

Maya doesn't dare go to the hospital because it is considered shameful and inappropriate to speak to anyone about sexual matters. It would be unthinkable to explain what has happened to her to a stranger, a man, an authority figure, or someone who is all three of these.

Not only does Maya fear being blamed for the rape, but she fears that no one will believe her or that people will think she is falsely accusing her attacker. They may think that perhaps she is pregnant and wants to hide her infidelity. She fears that if she tells her husband, he will never love her again, that he will abandon her, and that no one else will ever want to marry her. Maya fears that if her father finds out, he will cast her out of the family as ruined property. There are no witnesses to the rape, so Maya tells no one.

Maya is also traumatized: Her body and spirit have been brutally violated. She may have symptoms of post-traumatic stress disorder (PTSD), such as selective or incomplete memory, blocking out of painful events, and the inability to describe what has happened to her coherently and chronologically. She may be experiencing flashbacks, panic attacks, depression, anxiety, rage, nightmares, loss of appetite, difficulty sleeping, and other manifestations of her trauma. She may become totally withdrawn, be mistrustful of strangers, of family, of everyone. She may have an intense fear of authority and difficulty making eye contact, particularly with men.

Imagine that Maya and her husband fled their country a year ago and are now living in a refugee camp where they do not feel safe either. The suffocating misery of Maya and her husband's daily lives in the camp is too much for them to bear. They were lucky enough to get an interview with the United Nations High Commissioner for Refugees (UNHRC) so they can ask to be resettled in the United States to join Maya's sister and her family. They will have to explain to UNHCR how they have been persecuted, and they must convince them that they deserve resettlement and can neither return to their country nor continue to live in the refugee camp.

The interviewer asks Maya's husband about their situation. He describes how armed insurgents stormed their home two years ago, forcing them to flee for their lives. He describes their lives in the camp. He explains that he can't find work and that their children are in danger of starvation. They know people who have been threatened, even beaten, because they worked for the former government, as Maya's husband did. While Maya's husband speaks for both of them, the interviewer doesn't ask Maya any questions. The translator speaks a different dialect than Maya and her husband speak, and sometimes Maya is not sure if he is translating her husband's answers accurately to the interviewer.

After an hour, when the interview with Maya's husband has ended, the interviewer speaks directly to Maya for the first time. Does she wish to add anything? Maya is suddenly afraid that their case might be denied and that this is her only chance to speak. They are one family among so many; why should they be special? She is the only one who knows what happened to her. What will happen now if she reveals her rape not only to these two strange men but to her husband, who has never heard about it? What if he is horrified and furious that she has shamed him in front of these two strangers? But how can she live in fear in the refugee camp for the rest of her life? She has to tell someone. Should she tell her mother? Would her mother understand? Maybe she should risk telling her husband. Maybe, against all odds, he will understand and have compassion for her. Or should she ask for more time to think? She can always tell the interviewers that she forgot something and use the intervening time to tell the story to her mother. But what if they think she is lying, making the story up to help their case? What if they are still denied resettlement even though she has revealed the rape? Then she will be even worse off. Finally she makes a decision. "No," she says quietly and shakes her head.

Now consider an alternate scenario. Maya's husband has been killed, and she has no choice but to flee her country. She is terrified that her attacker will find her and rape her again and that there will be no end to these attacks. Maya manages to escape to the United States with the help of generous family friends who are able to procure a passport and visa for her. She believes that she will finally be safe in the United States and looks forward to living with a cousin who has agreed to take her in. Emotionally exhausted, still reeling from the trauma of the rape, the death of her husband, and the perilous flight from her country, she is fearful that she will be stopped when her plane lands, questioned, and forced to explain her most intimate experiences and fears to a complete stranger through a translator who may be a man. She is also apprehensive about starting her life over in a country whose language and culture are entirely foreign to her. She is lucky, however; much to her relief, she is allowed to enter the country.

Maya wants to apply for political asylum, but she does not have any money to pay a lawyer. When some of her cousin's friends advise her that a lawyer is unnecessary, she applies alone and unassisted for asylum with the Immigration and Naturalization Service (INS). She has decided that she has no choice but to explain about the rape, but she is very nervous during her interview with the INS. Her case is denied. The INS says she has provided insufficient detail about the events in her home country and no evidence to support her claim of rape. Moreover, she did not show that she was persecuted on account of her race, religion, nationality, membership in a particular social group, or political opinion, as required by law.

Maya now must present her asylum case before a judge in Immigration Court. From the time she was young, she was taught not to look men directly in the eye and certainly not to speak about personal things to them. But Maya must again explain about the rape. It is all a blur and very hard for her to talk about. She sobs when the INS and the judge ask her to describe what happened. They request details: dates, times, places. She begins frantically converting dates from her own calendar, but now she can't remember. Wait. She thinks she can remember what he said to her. But they are not satisfied. They want to know how she responded to him, and she doesn't know. How could she not know? She says he spoke to her only once. But before, she said it was twice. Which was it? Now she doesn't even remember what he said anymore. She is confused. Wait, she forgot some details. Can she ask the judge for a few minutes to collect her thoughts? Then the judge asks, Why were you raped?

Why was she raped? She doesn't understand the question. Was she raped because of her political opinion, her social group, her religion, her nationality, her race? She doesn't know. Did the officer say anything to her? Did he use derogatory names? Was he from a different ethnic group? Would he have known that they were of different ethnicities? How would he have known? Was he punishing her for that? Or was it "just a rape"? Did he just decide to rape her because he came upon her when she was alone and no one was looking? Does she know? How does she know? Does she have any evidence that she was actually raped? Did she go to the police? Is there a police report? Why not? Why didn't she go to the hospital? Does she have any medical records? Did she become pregnant? Were there any witnesses? Did she tell anyone? Why not?

Finally, Maya tries to explain that there is no city in her native country where she will be safe. How does she know she wouldn't be safe? Did she ever try to flee to another city? Did her attacker follow her there? Why didn't she try to flee if she was no longer safe? Why didn't she tell her husband?

Maya's only evidence is her word. However, in all asylum cases an applicant must prove the following and offer as much objectively verifiable evidence as possible: a well-founded fear of persecution by the government, or by a group that the government is unable or unwilling to control, on account of one's (1) race, (2) religion, (3) political opinion, (4) nationality, or (5) membership in a particular social group. An applicant also must prove that if persecuted by a nongovernment agent, he or she cannot relocate to any other part of his or her country safely. In addition, an applicant who has fled his or her country and has lived somewhere else before seeking asylum in the United States must prove that that country is equally unsafe. Perhaps the most important aspect of an asylum applicant's case is proving that he or she is credible.

For women who are facing gender-based persecution, these legal elements pose unique challenges. At first glance, it may appear as if her situation does not quite fit the legal requirements. Yet the policy behind refugee and asylum protection is for a foreign government to step in as a surrogate to protect a refugee from persecution where his or her own government has refused or failed to do so. This policy supports the protection of Maya and of other women who endure systemic violence because they are female.

The most patent obstacle for a woman who is seeking asylum because she is a woman—in the case of rape, domestic violence, or an honor crime, for example—is the fact that "gender" or "sex" is not listed as one of the accepted grounds for asylum. Therefore, women must fit their claims into one of the five grounds enumerated earlier, such as religion, membership in a particular social group, or political opinion. Obviously, it may be impossible for a rape survivor to prove that her persecutor was motivated by one of these factors. If Maya was raped by a police officer of a rival ethnic faction, his onetime use of a racial or ethnic slur, her memory of this, and her ability to recount it may be the only evidence she has to offer.

Often, women are fleeing from violence perpetrated by a family member. Typically, such violence is a systemic practice that is tolerated and even condoned and encouraged within the woman's society. For example, Maya feared that her husband or her father would kill her because of the rape. Other common examples of family-inflicted violence include female genital mutilation, forced marriage, incest, and domestic violence. A woman in one of these situations must prove that her government will not or cannot protect her from her family member. Proving this may be difficult, particularly if her country has laws on the books that criminalize the persecution. The woman must prove that the laws are not meaningfully enforced, but evidence is mostly anecdotal. By contrast, men rarely base an asylum case on persecution at the hands of family or tribal elders.

Obviously, if a woman like Maya faces severe repercussions for revealing what has happened to her, she will be deterred from presenting her case at all. Further, Maya's PTSD symptoms—confusion, nervousness, and selective memory—make her appear less credible once she does decide to testify about the rape. Ironically, a judge who is not well versed in typical manifestations of PTSD may interpret these symptoms as signs of dishonesty.[2]

Other obstacles besetting a woman may arise when her case is subsumed in her husband's, as when Maya and her husband were interviewed together by UNHCR. The woman may have suffered persecution that she has not told him about, and either she is never asked directly and her husband speaks for her, or she does not want to talk about it in front of him. In this particular situation, her case never gets heard even though it may be stronger than her husband's case.

CONCLUSION

Despite these many challenges, meaningful strides have been made recently in the legal field toward recognizing that violence against women—because they are women—often occurs within different contexts than violence against men. For example, in recent years, women facing honor crimes and domestic violence have brought increasingly successful asylum claims in the United States and in other refugee recipient countries. In addition, UNHCR has developed a "Women at Risk" program, which is designed to identify women who are in dire need of resettlement—such as widows or orphaned girls. In turn, more women have become hopeful that they may challenge the inevitability of violence on a daily basis.

It is clear, however, that if the legal system is to be an enabler of justice for women rather than a barrier to justice, lawmakers and adjudicators must take a much deeper look at the root causes of gender-based violence, that is, violence against women *because they are women*. Therefore, it is up to all people, regardless of ethnicity, religion, age, or nationality, to give voice to women and girls around the globe who have been silenced. For their sake, I hope this letter will reach you.

NOTES

1. The Center's project began as a collaborative endeavor with the Feminist Majority Foundation's (FMF) Campaign to Stop Gender Apartheid in Afghanistan. The Center served as a legal advisor to the FMF, participating alongside the FMF in meetings at the White House, with the State Department, Immigration and Naturalization Service, and United Nations High Commissioner for Refugees. Additionally, the FMF referred Afghan women facing persecution to the Center for legal representation.

2. A resourceful lawyer would submit to the immigration judge supporting documentation and evidence about Maya's country, its customs and about PTSD in rape survivors to help corroborate the facts. A lawyer would also encourage Maya to seek counseling, and she could help Maya overcome some of her reticence about testifying about the rape. Without such legal representation, however, Maya's chances of obtaining asylum are very slim.

PUBLIC HEALTH

A RECONSTRUCTION
PRIORITY IN AFGHANISTAN

ZOHRA RASEKH

NUMEROUS FACTORS HAVE CONTRIBUTED to the virtual destruction of the health infrastructure in Afghanistan: over two decades of war and internal conflict; the Taliban regime, particularly their policies toward women; the consequent crumbling of the economy; the drought; decades of inadequate investment in the country's healthcare sector; and the continuous drain of health personnel to other countries. Many Afghans suffer from preventable health problems, but they have little or no access to quality healthcare services. According to United Nations estimates, Afghanistan suffers from the highest level of disease and disability and has the second highest mortality rate in the world.[1]

Some of the major causes of the high morbidity and mortality rates are diarrhea, pneumonia, vaccine-preventable diseases, malaria, and malnutrition. Mortality among young women is mostly due to problems associated with pregnancy and labor. Tuberculosis kills 12,000 people every year. During March 2002, the National Tuberculosis Institute of the Ministry of Public Health reported 335 cases of this disease, 224 of which were women. The situation is especially severe in the rural areas, where there is immense poverty; poor environmental sanitation and personal hygiene; unsafe drinking water and insufficient food. Epidemics of infectious diseases like measles have been raging for many years in northern Afghanistan; they have claimed more than a thousand people, many of them children. This high death toll stems from the impossibility of getting medical help to the remote mountainous areas hardest hit by the epidemic.[2]

Of all the factors that have led to the failure of the health system in Afghanistan, the Taliban regime bears the greatest share of guilt, specifically in the areas of women's and children's health. In January 1997, Taliban officials announced a policy of segregating men and women into separate hospitals. Since the one "clinic" reserved for the half-million women of Kabul had never before been used as a hospital and had neither electricity nor running water, let alone medical supplies, this edict really meant the cessation of medical services for women. Besides shutting female patients out of the hospitals, the Taliban banned female hospital personnel, including physicians, nurses, pharmacists, and technicians, from working in any of Kabul's twenty-two hospitals. During this period, many women and young girls died from preventable illness and traumas.[3] As a result of international pressure, the Taliban authorities reopened a few hospitals for women, and female medical personnel were allowed to return to their jobs.[4]

But women had even less access to healthcare after the policy reversal than before. After September 1997, only 20 percent of hospital beds dedicated to adults were available for women. In addition, both medical personnel and supplies were severely limited.

In 1998, as part of my study of the health and human rights of Afghan women under the Taliban, I interviewed over 200 women in Kabul as well as in the Pakistan refugee community. One female physician mourned the death of a patient who was unable to go anywhere to obtain an insulin shot. Other cases included a young woman who was hit by a car and bled to death inside a taxi after she was rejected by several local hospitals. A twelve-year-old girl with measles died because the Taliban authorities would not allow a male pediatrician to attend to her in the children's ward, which was adjacent to the women's ward.

The physical condition of women was not the only aspect of their health to suffer. The participants in my study reported declining mental health as well. Many were showing symptoms of psychiatric disorders. Overall, 81 percent of respondents in Kabul reported a decline in their mental health during the previous year, and 35 percent reported that their mental conditions significantly interfered with daily activities. Based on self-reported symptoms, 42 percent of respondents met the diagnostic criteria for post-traumatic stress disorder (PTSD), over 95 percent met the criteria for major depression, and 86 percent demonstrated significant symptoms of anxiety. Among the participants, 20 percent reported that they had thoughts of attempting suicide. "I have no income and no one to support my family. Often when my children ask for food, I beat them. I feel like killing all my children and killing myself. I can't bear the pressure any more," said a young widow, the mother of five children.[5] Notwithstanding this epidemic of mental illnesses, mental health services are virtually nonexistent. As of May 2002, one mental health facility with fifty beds and no trained personnel exists for the total population of Kabul. While this situation seems dire for both men and women, women are still at a disadvantage. Only twenty of the fifty beds are reserved for them; they still have limited access to the facility; and mental illness among women is soaring as a result of the suffering they endured during the Taliban regime.

In January 2001, a fact-finding team from Global Watch Group (GWG) visited the northern regions of Afghanistan to assess the health conditions of internally displaced people (IDPs). Many Afghans, who were fleeing the war, the Taliban, and years of drought, were forced to live in exile in this region. Near the northern villages of Khoja Bhawahuddin and Dosht-e-Qala, thousands of families were living in makeshift tent homes in camps without access to basic medical services.

In the Panjshir Valley, many displaced persons lived in crudely built shelters with poor sanitation and far from medical facilities. The existing government-supported village clinics lacked essential medicine and supplies. The few medical facilities supported by nongovernmental organizations (NGOs) were also sparsely equipped and poorly attended. Many people were ill and dying of potentially curable acute respiratory disease and diarrheal illness. Other diseases, including malaria, tuberculosis, typhoid, and measles had been reported in the camps.

Months after the fall of the Taliban, Afghanistan still needs immeasurable aid—starting with safe food and drinking water. A system to provide these essentials and to control infectious disease outbreaks is lacking; diseases such as polio and tuberculosis are on the rise. The general population, which has a high rate of illiteracy, needs to be educated about basic public health measures such as personal hygiene and sanitation.

GWG's needs assessment of healthcare in the cities of Kabul and Herat in the winter and spring of 2002 indicates that despite the monetary contributions promised by the international community for the reconstruction of the country, neither the interim government nor international organizations have developed a plan to meet the urgent short-term healthcare needs of the Afghan people. Although conditions for women have improved in terms of their mobility in public places, access to education, and the dress code, their health remains very poor. Reproductive and mental health problems are the worst in a long list of critical health issues. Women die from preventable complications during pregnancy and delivery. In Kabul, I interviewed the family of a young woman who died from postnatal infection. Another pregnant woman was at risk of losing her unborn baby due to heavy housework and sexual contact with her husband during the late stages of pregnancy.

Currently, the majority of people, including IDPs, still have no access even to a poor-quality healthcare facility. Since the four provinces surrounding the city of Herat (Farah, Badghees, Neemroze, and Ghore) have no clinics, people in need of medical care have to travel to Herat, other Afghan cities, and in some cases outside the country to seek help.

Herat itself, one of the largest cities in Afghanistan, has only one hospital, poorly equipped with a capacity of 200 beds (used as 400 beds) serving an estimated 5 million people: 2.5 million from Herat and nearly 3 million from the 4 provinces. This hospital operates with partial electricity, no running water, unsanitary conditions, no laboratories, worn-out beds, no bedding (patients have to bring their own), no medical or surgical equipment, meager supplies of lifesaving antibiotics and other drugs, and poorly trained staff. According to local physicians, patients die from treatable diseases and preventable problems. For example, patients in diabetic crisis die every day because there is no refrigeration for storing insulin.

In general, patient care has come to be a guessing game mainly because of poor quality medical education and a scarcity of medical personnel and diagnostic tools. "I haven't seen an X-ray machine in my life and most medical students don't know what a microscope looks like," said Dr. Aman Sameem, an internist in one of Kabul's local hospitals. Like most other physicians, Dr. Sameem graduated from Kabul University Medical School and was trained in local hospitals, where medical equipment and supplies are scarce or unavailable altogether.

Disabilities due to land mines, bombs, rocket attacks, and corporal punishment by the Taliban, such as beatings and limb amputations, were among the most visible public health problems in Kabul and Herat. The recent bombings by the U.S. military have disabled many men, women, and children. In a Kabul trauma hospital run by an Italian NGO, seven children who lost their legs as a result of the U.S. bombings during the previous few months were recovering from injuries and surgical procedures.

THE ROLE OF PUBLIC HEALTH IN THE RECONSTRUCTION OF AFGHANISTAN

Generally, "public health" is an unfamiliar term to most people in Afghanistan, even to healthcare workers themselves. But without improvements in this area, Afghans may not be able to participate effectively in developing a sustainable economy, security, and peace. At the moment, reducing the unacceptably high levels of poverty, mortality, morbidity, and disability in the shortest possible period of time should be among the top priorities of reconstruction efforts. Given the limited human resources and financial constraints, immediate attention should focus on healthcare gaps in the areas of mental health, reproductive health, and disability. Meanwhile, a long-term nationwide action plan needs to be developed and implemented. This must include appropriate management systems, such as a reliable salary scale for health workers. At the time of my January 2002 visit, healthcare workers had not received salary for six months.

Short-term objectives must include:

- Nationwide maternal and child health services to reduce the high levels of maternal and infant mortality
- Nationwide mental health services
- Reviving existing local hospitals and physiotherapy centers by providing necessary medical and orthopedic equipment and drug supplies
- Training and deployment of medical personnel in all areas of healthcare, including traditional birth attendants and specialists in obstetrics, tuberculosis specialists, and mental health counselors
- Control and prevention of infectious diseases such as measles, cholera, tuberculosis, malaria, meningitis, hepatitis, typhoid, childhood respiratory infections, diarrhea
- HIV/AIDS education and awareness for school children, government employees, policy makers, healthcare providers, returning refugees, and others
- Alleviation of high levels of malnutrition.

Long-term objectives include:

- Nationwide public health system
- Schools of public health
- A health information system using radio, TV, Internet, newsletters, and community and religious centers
- Training and deployment of medical personnel in all areas of healthcare, including traditional birth attendants and specialists in obstetrics, tuberculosis specialists, and mental health counselors
- Clean water supplies and sanitation facilities
- Family planning programs
- HIV/AIDS education and awareness
- Clearing and elimination of land mines and other unexploded ordnances.

CONCLUSION

Dealing with the dire physical and mental problems currently afflicting the Afghan people and establishing a new public health system are the most urgent tasks among a formidable list of goals for Afghan reconstruction. If the healthcare needs of the population are not addressed, the other goals cannot be properly implemented. Consider these grim statistics: Life expectancy at birth is forty-four years. One in four children dies before age five, one in twelve women dies in childbirth, and the population growth rate is over 3 percent.[6] No improvements—economic, social, educational—will help the country without a concomitant improvement in public health. The population will be either too ill or too diminished to participate in the rebuilding of their homeland. As the international community assesses its contributions to the future of Afghanistan, public health must be placed at the very top of the list.

NOTES

1. From Center for Economic and Social Rights (CESR). For these statistics and further information about health issues in Afghanistan, see www. CESR.org, Report, "Human Rights and Reconstruction in Afghanistan."

2. Global Watch Group interview with the Deputy Minister of Health, Kabul, Afghanistan, February 2002.
3. Vincent Iacopino, Zohra Rasekh, et al. *The Taliban's War on Women: A Health and Human Rights Crisis in Afghanistan* (Physicians for Human Rights), 1998.
4. Medicins Sans Frontières, "Consequences of the New Public Health Policy Decisions Regarding Female Healthcare in Kabul, Afghanistan," report published by MSF office in Kabul, 1997.
5. This interview and similar interviews discussed in Iacopino, passim.
6. CESR.

TWO IDENTITIES, ONE MISSION

FARIBA NAWA

SEPTEMBER 11, 2001, SERVED as a critical turning point in an odyssey I have been on as long as I can remember. I was born in Herat, Afghanistan, on the day King Mohammad Zahir Shah was ousted in 1973. My family fled the Soviet war in Afghanistan twenty years ago, and we moved to the insular Afghan community in Fremont, California, where my parents still live. I grew up in the Bay Area suburb straddling two cultures, one embedded in Islam and family and the other founded on American values of secular individualism.

Melding my dual identities had always been an issue for me, at the very least an abstract and intellectual challenge. But the September 11 attacks catapulted my struggle to center stage.

I am a freelance journalist and a Near Eastern Studies master's student at New York University, living in the heart of an Arab neighborhood. At 9 A.M. on September 11, I reached for my cell phone, half awake, to call an office a few blocks away from the World Trade Center. I needed to pick up some documents for a class. I heard a deafening out-of-service noise. Cursing the local phone company, I curled back up in bed when my roommate's brother knocked on the door and asked me to come up to the roof.

There, across the East River four miles away, the Twin Towers were in flames. I stood silent, in shock. My instant fear was that the next site of destruction would be Afghanistan. And indeed, in less than a month, my two countries were at war.

From the age of ten until I finished college, I struggled to define and come to terms with my hyphenated identity. With blond hair and an American accent, I had no problems fitting into my suburban school—on a superficial level. But on a deeper level, I felt isolated and misunderstood. My classmates sneered when I spoke my native Persian. They said I was weird for skipping school dances to attend family parties. They could not understand why family would have more centrality than school friends since they themselves were going through the typical American adolescent process of breaking away from family and prioritizing peer relationships. Few had ever heard of Afghanistan or understood its culture.

Then at home my mother said I wasn't a "good Afghan girl" when I joined friends on outings and stayed over at slumber parties. She didn't like me tweezing my eyebrows because in Afghan culture unmarried girls are not supposed to remove their facial hair. For me, these two identities existed side by side in an uneasy but workable truce.

I returned to my birthplace in 2000 after nineteen years in exile. Afghanistan was in the midst of a drought, starvation, and civil war between the Taliban and the Northern Alliance. With a Taliban-issued Afghan passport, I donned the *burqa*, the all-enveloping garment my mother used to wear, and spent seven days with "Bibi"—my precious grandmother—and my other relatives in Herat.

I first rode a decorated Toyota Corolla taxi, then a horse-drawn wagon to reach my family home. I knocked at the old brass gate. I was going to surprise Bibi. A child opened the door and led me to my grandmother. She was praying. I lifted the front of my *burqa* as she turned her head. My seventy-year-old grandmother screamed in disbelief. She passed out for a few seconds before hugging me and sobbing on my shoulders. Then she gave me a tour of what remained of my paternal home.

Most of the original place had been sold and was now being used for storing tires. I didn't care much because my memories of the house were filled with death and war. At my elementary school across the street, I had once witnessed my second-grade classmates die under bombs.

My memories of a happy childhood were about my maternal grandfather's orchard home, where my cousins and I had played. The house stood next to the sports stadium where the Taliban staged their public executions. When I returned there, I stepped into the orchard, threw my *burqa* to the ground, and sprinted toward the living quarters, hearing my family's laughter inside the hallways.

But the doors to the seven rooms were locked, and some of the windows broken. I ran out to the field, searching for the mulberry and pomegranate trees where we used to picnic. I found the trees, but they bore no fruit because of the drought. The entire place seemed much smaller than I remembered until I recalled hearing that my uncles had sold three acres.

I climbed the roof overlooking the city and wept. The tears were a catharsis, an acceptance of the past as past. My distance from Herat for these nineteen years had left a void in me. I missed something as I had lived my comfortable Western life in Fremont. But 10,000 miles away, leaning at the edge of my childhood roof, I felt a sense of completion.

During the rest of my trip, my Herati cousins and I enjoyed each other. My cousins were rebellious and ignored the Taliban's hard-line prohibitions. We sang, danced, watched satellite television, and shopped at jewelry stores. I had heard that women could not leave their homes without a male kin, but the streets were filled with *burqa*-clad women walking on their own.

Heratis were both afraid and defiant of the Taliban, who were Pashto speakers occupying an ancient and cultured Persian-speaking city.[1] Their extreme version of Islam was foreign to the urban Heratis. Since the port of Herat was the Taliban's base for money, they gave its residents more freedom than they gave others, and Heratis took advantage of it in a schizophrenic manner. My cousins would drum on their tambourines at midnight, cursing the Taliban as they sang. The next day the girls whispered in conversation, afraid the Taliban were coming to get them. Despite all the conflict, I left Herat with a feeling that I had reached full circle.

What I discovered on this trip was how comfortable I had become with my duality, how easily I could slip between the lifestyles in Herat and Fremont.

I embody what many Westerners and Muslims see as a clash of civilizations: Islam versus the West. Indeed, the belief that there is a clash of civilizations has become the driving force in contemporary politics. The ideology expounded by scholar Samuel Huntington has been exploited by American pundits and by fanatics like Osama bin Laden to pit the Western and Muslim worlds against each other. Simply stated, the idea proposes that the two cultures cannot reconcile their religious and secular differences, and, in the end, one has to conquer the other.

Over the years, I developed a philosophy of my own. I had come to believe that this "clash" simplifies the complexities and diversity of humanity. Perhaps as a result of an economic need for competition, the United States—the leader of the West—needs to create an adversary, an "other." After the fall of the Soviet Union and the end of the Cold War, the new "other" became the Islamic belt and its one billion people. The media spread the government's and the corporate world's polarizing definitions, and Muslims themselves fell victim to them. Fanaticism practiced by groups like the Taliban is a symptom of such myopic thought.

The Taliban are believers in the "clash of civilizations" because they demonize Western secularism and see the end of history in the West's twisted interpretation of Islam. It became clear to me during my trip that although the West with its "corrupt values" was the prime target of Taliban rage and hostility, their ultimate agenda had little to do with Islam. Islam was being used as an excuse to crush any culture and identity different from theirs.

This realization supported my growing belief that there was no fundamental and irreconcilable clash of cultures and values. I had gradually reached the conclusion that culture is fluid, changing rapidly in every society. I had traveled to other Muslim countries, including Egypt, Pakistan, and Iran, and I had seen the similarity of both worlds in their quest for fulfillment.

What I had reconciled came crashing down as the World Trade Center crumbled. I could not lie to myself. There was a clash of civilizations taking place, not, however, in the realm of ideology, but in the more terrifying realm of practical reality. My own personal perspective was no longer important. Those who did see the world in terms of Islam versus the West had managed to terrorize and divide the planet. Their viewpoint may be false, their ideology may be a farce, rooted in hegemonic tradition, but I had to face the frightening facts that not only do many ignorant individuals take the idea of a conflict between Islam and the West seriously, but they act on it, making it real and unyielding.

Like so many Americans, I asked myself what I should do now. And like other Afghan Americans, I asked myself how I could bridge the gap between the two worlds.

I did not have to anguish over my role for long. Although I had written about Afghanistan and its people for ten years, calling for the world to pay attention to its plight after the Soviet withdrawal, few people had been interested in what I had to say. Now, after New York's day of infamy, when terrorist suspects became linked with Afghanistan, I—together with the entire Afghan community of exiles—suddenly became a media magnet. For the first time, *everyone* seemed interested in what I had to say.

So I shared my views in the broadcast and print media for two weeks, explaining the intricate events spanning twenty-two years in Afghanistan. I was plugged in as "the Afghan voice," not as a Western-educated journalist. Americans trusted my Caucasian appearance.

"We need a character who's confident, speaks good English, and can deliver the information with drama," one television producer said to me.

Reality was dramatic enough. I did not need to generate any more drama. I felt I had a mission. It was as if all the strands of my life led to this moment, this opportunity for self-understanding and for disseminating information about Afghanistan to the West. On October 1, 2001, I gave up a $25,000 scholarship to take the semester off. I packed my tape recorder, notebooks, and pens and took a three-month job as a stringer for Agence France Presse in Islamabad.

But the decision to give up my brownstone home, my scholarship, and my safety did not come easily. My fears were compounded by a troubling omen. A week before I left, I had asked my spiritual aunt to recite a special prayer. The prayer is intended to provide assistance in making difficult decisions. The answer to the dilemma is supposed to come in a dream. My aunt, who lives in Hawaii, called me a week after her prayer to stop me from going. She said she had dreamed of a foreign place where alligators were approaching her, but she was unable to escape them. She believed that this was a sign for me to stay in New York. But it was too late to change my mind. I had packed my bags and bought my plane tickets. I could not turn back now.

I was dreaming of bullets raining from the sky when the U.S.-led attack began in Afghanistan. The rest of October is hazy in my mind. I worked fourteen-hour days, churning out breaking news, talking to commanders on front lines via satellite telephones, and meeting Afghan refugees and power brokers in Peshawar.

My identity issues rose to the fore throughout this time, as I felt forced to choose sides when I interviewed politicians, military experts, and Afghan refugees. They looked at me with curiosity and suspicion. Some asked, "Who are you for?" My standard answer was, "I'm for peace and democracy."

The stories I wrote haunted my dreams.

The starving refugee I interviewed turned into my sister at night. I saw blistered feet and heard her wince because, after days of walking, she was too tired to make it to the border. The faint racket of helicopters passing my Islamabad house became an unbearable clamor in my sleep. I saw a wide-eyed seven-year-old girl lying on desert dunes gazing at the sky as rockets dropped all around her. When I woke up sweating, I remembered that when I was seven, Soviet helicopters rushed through Herat for an entire day heading toward the villages for combat with mujahideen guerillas. The dreams were twisted flashbacks combining the current situation with the war I witnessed during the Soviet invasion.

I had an advantage because I speak Persian and know the region's history. But I was also at a disadvantage because with each breaking news event, my emotions fluctuated between glee when I heard that the Taliban were losing, and sadness when I heard the civilian death tolls. On some days I had hope and courage; on others I was filled with despair and terror. As bombs fell on major cities, I prayed that my grandmother and great-uncles would survive in Herat. Although a reporter is supposed to be objective, I had no distance from the news.

I had a recurring dream in which my beautiful blue-eyed grandmother, with tears running down her face, held out the edge of her sheer white headscarf and asked me to take it. I tried to grab the fabric, but my Bibi turned into a shadow and disappeared. I screamed and kept running after her but could not catch up.

The dream is a disturbing echo of reality. I have not heard from my grandmother since American planes bombed my birthplace, but I learned from relatives in Pakistan that Bibi survived. That's not good enough for me. I want to hold her in my arms. I want to hug her. I want to promise her that Herat will be safe from now on.

Once the Northern Alliance swept through the north, the popular mujahideen governor Ismail Khan recaptured Herat. I was anxious to visit Afghanistan in person, but I had to wait for appropriate visas to be prepared and approved. Meanwhile, unexpectedly, Pakistan declared me persona non grata, refusing a visa extension on my American passport and ordering my immediate departure.

To this day, I do not understand why the Pakistani authorities took this action. Was it because I had lunch with an Indian journalist? Was it because I was in touch with Northern Alliance commanders who shunned Pakistan's influence? Was it because I can cross over between the two worlds of Islam and the West so comfortably? Whatever the reason, the official story was that I was, in the words of the country's interior ministry, a "detriment to Pakistan." I was deported before any other bordering nation could grant me a visa. Of course, my work contract was breached because I could no longer cover the war on location.

Instead of returning to New York, I went to Bonn, Germany, to cover the historic United Nations talks on Afghanistan. For the first time, I saw Afghan leaders forced to work out their differences and sign an agreement paving the way for free elections and democracy. It certainly provided me with much-needed relief from the bombings and atrocities. But the real impact of the conference on my psyche took place at a deeper level. Foreign powers pressured the Afghan leaders to draft the agreement. And the United States no longer considered Afghanistan a threat, so the once-rogue nation was no longer classified in the "them" category.

The success of Bonn served as proof to me that there is no clash between Muslims and the West when it is in no one's interest to put the "us versus them" theory into practice. It validated the stance I had taken prior to September 11 and went a long way toward helping me sort out the identity issues that had overwhelmed me.

But Afghanistan's burgeoning peace and democracy were a small victory. The "us versus them" mentality still lingers, only it has taken a different form. President George W. Bush boosted his popularity by simplifying it into a good versus evil battle. And the militant Islamists are returning the call for revenge as they recruit more angry young Muslims into Al Qaeda. The U.S.-led war on terrorism ultimately will breed worse "terrorists" than we have ever seen.

We need to find ways to learn and understand what seems most different and intolerable. As a member of the media who has the vantage point of both civilizations, I am searching for solutions that embrace the complexity of each civilization and seek to bridge gaps rather than play on stereotypes, oversimplified dichotomies, and people's deep-seated fear and distrust.

As reconstruction begins in my homeland, the media and thus the world will soon shift their attention to the next global crisis. But my own focus will remain on Afghanistan as I return to write about redevelopment. My first priority is to find my Bibi, hold her in my arms, and fall asleep peacefully.

NOTES

1. The two main languages of Afghanistan are Pashto, which is spoken by Pashtuns, and Dari. Dari, which is classical Persian (Farsi), originated in what is now northeast Afghanistan but was once part of the Persian Empire.

HOPE IN AFGHANISTAN

MASUDA SULTAN

AT FIRST, MAMOON REMINDED me of a mouse. His head was a little big for his tiny six-year-old frame, and his eyes always seemed to be looking for something to play with as they darted from one object to another. The youngest of six siblings, he ran around my aunt's house poking the other children, peering back at me as he did so, waiting for me to stop him from being a nuisance. Playfully I gave him a poke instead of a scold, and he burst out laughing, revealing a huge smile of tiny teeth. He could see I was willing to play his game.

It was late July in 2001, and I was nearly two weeks into my journey. This was the first time I had been in Afghanistan since my family fled when I was Mamoon's age. I was twenty-three now, the same age as the war.

I was in the Taliban-controlled city of Kandahar as guest of my mother's older sister. It was several weeks before the towers were to fall, still the time when Afghanistan was forgotten by the world. I had come in through the Pakistani city of Quetta, driving six hours on mostly unpaved roads to explore my roots, visit the relatives we had left behind, and also explore the option of working in a humanitarian organization in Kandahar, where my family had lived for as many generations as we could count.

Their home was a typical Afghan residence build around a courtyard. It was badly decayed; there were bullet holes in the walls and half of it had been closed off because it was unlivable. The family couldn't afford to rebuild it because they were just getting by on what relatives were sending them from the United States.

Twenty-five years ago, my mother's older sister had married and moved into this house. We call her Khala Sherina, which means "sweet aunt" in Pashto.[1] Her given name is Spoozhmai—"moon." Since her marriage, her only travel had been a recent visit to her nieces and nephews in Pakistan. Her sister, my oldest aunt, had passed away there while carrying her fifth child.

Khala Sherina shot Mamoon a look of motherly discipline when he poked me back. Mamoon dropped his arms by his side and then froze. An apologetic expression came over his face. Khala Sherina embraced me, then turned to Mamoon. "Do you know what a valuable guest this is?"

I looked at Khala Sherina's warm smile. In her youth, she must have been stunning. Even now, in her off-white dress printed with autumn flowers, she looked almost like a girl. Only the wrinkles surrounding her eyes and lips gave away her age. Her hair, adorned by a single pin, had recently been dyed jet black in anticipation of her guests. She wore it short. In America we say she had a trendy bob, but this was the hairstyle she had worn all her life. My arrival had been a surprise to her. She had been expecting only her youngest sister, Karimah. I'm the daughter of Runa, her second youngest sister.

As Khala Sherina explained who I was, Mamoon perched on a red velvet mattress on the floor. She told him she hadn't seen me since I was four years old. Mamoon knew I had come from America, but he was more interested in the fact that there was someone new for him to focus his curiosity on. It was the young adults and older people who were fascinated by my having become an American.

To Khala Sherina and my other relatives, my first return meant everything. They regarded me with such respect—almost awe—that I felt embarrassed. They treated me as if I were better than they just because I had come from America. They insisted that I have the best seat on the floor during meals. They insisted that I take my food before the children took theirs. I wasn't allowed to wash dishes or help with any other domestic duties. They even tried to launder my clothes. My cousin Ousi, who is around my age, mothered me. At night, we slept under mosquito nets on mattresses in the open courtyard of the house. Ousi made sure my mosquito net was doubly tucked in and safe from breach before settling in next to me, ready to assist me at night if I needed something as there was no electric light. When I needed to bathe, she filled buckets from the artesian well and carried them upstairs for me. She didn't want me to have too hard a time adjusting to the way they lived.

Her enthusiasm to be my guide and protector was both sweet and funny. One night she asked me if I was scared of the dark. I shot her a look of reassurance and told her how tough I was. After all, I had grown up in Brooklyn and Queens. America had not softened me *that* much. That night we laughed together like sisters.

To Afghans, America is an almost mythical place, reached only by people with strong initiative and great luck. As they see it, people who make it to America leap into a higher class. This is especially true for women. For women who visit Afghanistan after moving to America, going back is an opportunity to be a star. Everyone dotes on them. People envy them because they drive automobiles and can afford to buy jewelry and stylish clothes. American women own luxuries like washing machines and microwave ovens. Americans are the stars of the world, and to walk among them makes Afghans likewise stellar. Reaching American shores holds the same allure and mystique for Afghans as Hollywood celebrity holds for Americans.

I did my best to downplay my American privilege. I followed my mother's advice and wore nothing nicer than the clothing my hosts wore. I didn't bring my best clothes, and I certainly did not bring American clothes. I wore no jewelry. Apparently I disappointed my relatives, who expected nothing short of grandeur. They poked fun of my plain black Aerosole flats. Ironically, they looked more fashionable than I did and were a little confused because the American had not swept in clad in elegant regalia.

When I visited Janaraa, one of my mother's cousins, she picked up my shoes and looked at them with distaste. "I would never be caught wearing these," she quipped.

Janaraa was a plain woman in her forties. She had some gray hairs and, more important, little fear of expressing how she felt. She is one of the most outgoing women I met in Afghanistan. She usually spikes her words with humor and is adept at using her wit to say things she might not get away with otherwise.

"Do you have such a low a opinion of our sense of fashion that you dress this way to visit us? If you send gifts, don't send ones like this."

My austerity stemmed from something I felt was more important than humility. I was afraid to show my relatives what they were missing by not being in the United States. Most Afghans feel they have been discarded by the world. But even though they remember that the United States abandoned them after the Soviets were driven out, they still want a chance at my lifestyle. Above all, they want opportunity. All the Afghans I met wanted desperately to make it to America. During private moments, even the proudest of them confided that they would leave for America immediately if they could.

For most Afghans this desire sits quietly beneath their unflinchingly stoic exterior. When it is brought to the edge of their hearts, where they must acknowledge and confront it, they grow tortured with longing. I knew I would meet many people who would believe I could help them get to America. I represented the freedom and magic of the West. My visit was a tough reminder of a world they were excluded from. So I tried to minimize the extreme gap between my privilege and their reality.

Sulaiman, Janaraa's husband, hatched his own plan for making it to the United States. He was a handsome, jovial man with leathery skin, a button nose, and soft eyes. With my small video camera, Sulaiman recorded a marriage proposal to a very elderly cousin in the United States. At first I thought this was a joke, but he was serious. He would marry this cousin so he could come to America, and then he would send for Janaraa and the rest of his family. Janaraa joked that once Sulaiman got there, the elderly cousin wouldn't divorce him because she would want to keep him all to herself.

With Khala Sherina's home as my base, I made several trips to visit other family members. I journeyed between homes always under the cover of a *chadari* or *burqa,* the now-infamous garment that covers a woman from head to toe. The headpiece of the *chadari* has a mesh insert woven of heavy blue thread through which I could discern the world ahead of me in a blurred, stifled way. At all times I had to be accompanied by a male relative. Whenever I returned, I would find Mamoon running about the house, engaged in mischief. Usually I would play with him in the guest room, or what is the equivalent of a parlor in the West.

Khala Sherina would open this otherwise locked room to accommodate guests. Like the rest of the house, the room was constructed of adobe. There were no windows, and the walls were covered in a watery white paint. Several red velvet mattresses stuffed with sponge and feathers were spread on the floor for sitting.

The guest room held the family's most valuable possessions. There was the refrigerator, which, being locked away in the guest room, was across the courtyard, quite far from the kitchen. There was no furniture beyond the mattresses, though the walls had recessed shelves that held other family treasures. The peaked arches of these recesses, or *tagchas,* pointed skyward. In one of them matching cups circled a lime-green glass pitcher. Mounted in a gold frame above it, in elegant red and black script, was a prayer, which had been beautifully penned by Ousi's younger brother Homayoon, who was apprenticed to a calligrapher.

One of the exalted treasures in the room was a common soccer trophy. The base was plastic made to look like wood. The plastic figurine at the top reflected a dull gold light. Looking at the trophy, I felt as if I could have been standing in any living room in suburban America. Since sports were discouraged, if not occasionally outlawed by the Taliban, this item intrigued me.

It turned out that the trophy had been awarded to Najib, Mamoon's brother. At twenty-one, Najib looked like an older version of Mamoon except that his head was the right size for his body. He was slight—five feet four inches—polite and soft-spoken, though his big nostrils would flare when he talked to me.

Najib told me about his soccer trophy when we were traveling across rock-strewn roads in 100-degree heat to visit relatives. On that day Najib was my male escort. Though cousins could not serve as escorts under Taliban law because cousins can marry (fathers, brothers, and uncles could be escorts), we were prepared to lie and claim a brother-sister relationship if we were caught. He seemed ready to open up as we sat in the back of a shaky motorized rickshaw. As we rattled along, I could just barely make out the sun-bleached earth and the rocks, which were tinted blue by the screen of my *chadari*. I steadied myself on a metal stabilizer bar and listened.

Najib appeared nervous as he spoke, taking short, quick breaths between sentences. He told me he was a good soccer player. He believed that if only he had the chance to prove himself, this talent would be his ticket to success. He was not unlike thousands of American boys who dream of playing major league baseball or professional basketball. But Najib's aspirations were considerably more modest. They weren't about making it to the big leagues; they were about making it to America. In Afghanistan, America is the big league.

Najib knew that at one time I had worked for the Confederation of North, Central America and Caribbean Association Football (CON-CACAF), and he wanted me to use my soccer contacts to bring him to America. I watched his humility thin for a moment in the glaring sun. I was being pitched. It was painful to hear this modest man trying to sell himself. I wanted to help him.

He offered to play soccer on a trial basis, happily without pay. He believed that if only he could show his talent to the right people, he would make it in soccer and stay in the United States. I felt a lurch in my stomach, a silent emptiness, as he poured his hope into me. This responsibility made me uneasy, especially because he thought it was simple: just believe in him. I knew I couldn't make it happen. The contrast between the opportunities available in the United States and the limited possibilities open to Afghan youngsters filled me with sadness and helplessness. The reality was as harsh as the jerkily passing landscape.

Back at Khala Sherina's, I had gifts to give out. We were all seated in the guest room on the red velvet mattresses. By this time Mamoon and I had developed a friendship, so he sat next to me to help pass out the presents. He waited patiently and politely for his. As I looked at him, with his cowlick waving back and forth, I wanted to sink into the earth and fall through. I had no gift for Mamoon.

When the gifts had been handed out and he realized there was nothing for him, he looked at me with puzzled disappointment. I could have brought him something from my world, and I had failed. But I had just learned of Mamoon's existence on my arrival—one can't do anything for a person if one doesn't know he exists. To most of the world, I thought, Afghanistan really didn't exist either. Mamoon was an unknown child in a forgotten land. I had to travel thousands of miles, not knowing what to expect, to find this little kid to fall in love with.

The next morning I promised to take him to the market to buy him whatever he wanted, regardless of price. Khala Sherina thought I was being silly. She worried about me going to the marketplace with a little boy. The law required an adult male escort, but I was determined to make this trip with Mamoon.

The marketplace was a bazaar like something out of the *Arabian Nights*. There were street vendors everywhere hawking their wares, yelling at people to look at them, and then haggling with those who ventured over. People were shouting and pushing on us in the bustle. My *chadari* obscured my vision. I told Mamoon he had to hold my hand because I didn't know where I was going. He kept running ahead of me in his excitement, and I was afraid he would abandon me in this world I didn't understand. I was now dependent on this six-year-old mouse.

Soon I stopped and shouted, "Mamoon, you've got to come back and hold my hand!"

I told him I wasn't going to continue unless he led me. He turned back and shook his head, the cowlick springing back and forth. He came back, took my hand, and said to me, "Don't worry. Don't pay attention to the people yelling. Just follow me."

I began to see the grown-up side of this child.

He knew exactly where he wanted to go, and we soon arrived at one particular vendor who sold plastic trucks and other toy vehicles. The trucks were probably the cheapest, poorest-quality toys I had ever seen in my entire life. When Mamoon picked a little car, I thought, *That's it?* He could have anything he wanted, and he picked a very modest item from a very modest selection. I was disappointed. I wanted him to have something grander. His choice cost pennies.

I asked him if that was really what he wanted. Reluctantly, almost embarrassed, he pointed to the biggest truck the vendor had and said, "That's really what I want."

I told him to take it and pick out things for his brothers. We ended up buying a bagful. When it came time to pay, Mamoon became very protective as he was afraid I couldn't handle the transaction. I had no idea how much money I had, so I gave it all to him. After a discussion with the vendor, Mamoon carefully counted the money out.

Later, my family said the vendor had probably cheated me. Since I intentionally hadn't haggled, he may well have. But I didn't care. It was the first time I had dealt with a merchant in my native country, and I found it beautiful to be able to talk to him in my own Pashto and to buy these items in the bazaar. If he wanted to rip me off for a few pennies, that was my gift to him for the experience. My family laughed at me when I told them this. But at least this time they were laughing at something other than my shoes.

As I watched Mamoon's delight as he played with his new trucks, I realized he didn't have much else to do. There were no schools and only his siblings and occasional pesky cousins to play with. He was still young enough that the house appeared huge, and there was enough there to amuse him. But I knew he would soon become restless. While Mamoon was still curious about the things he could find in the family courtyard, his older siblings were listless from boredom, confinement, and lack of a vision. I recalled times during my childhood when I had to stay home because I was sick or because a vacation fell when my parents weren't available to take me anywhere and none of my friends were free. I remembered how the time crawled. And I was fortunate. I had books to read, video games, and a television set for amusement. My Afghan cousins had none of these. What if this monotony filled 365 days of the year? This was life for Mamoon's older siblings. It would soon be like this for Mamoon. He could attend a *madressa,* but his parents would rather he not be taught with Taliban texts. He would probably spend his whole life in and around this house.

Until I visited Khala Sherina and my other relatives, I had never seen people with so little give so much. I hadn't known that people who felt abandoned could be welcoming. Their generosity overwhelmed and moved me. Although I was in a modest home, I was treated like royalty. Cousins who had never met me related to me as their sister. Everyone, from Mamoon to his mother, protected me.

I saw courage and fearlessness in these people. I saw the courage brewing early in Mamoon when he realized he should protect and guide me through the marketplace. I remember seeing it in the men of my country as they boldly rode their motorcycles across the dusty and rocky terrain. They rode without helmets, the tails of their turbans tossed over their noses and mouths to protect them from the dust.

I wondered what they were thinking as they flew down dangerous roads. The rest of the world seemed not to exist; the only thing that mattered was the uncertain stretch before them. I thought they were at their most handsome then. These men may seem primitive to the rest of the world, but I realized that they have developed in a certain way because they have faced indescribable pain, most of which they may never tell.

Westerners have correctly focused on the oppression of women in Afghanistan, but they have not taken sufficient note of the anguish of Afghan men. It was from the women that I learned how much the men have been hurting. The wound of abandonment runs deep in them. Afraid to be vulnerable, fiercely independent, they hide their wounds. This is the way they have coped with unspeakable hardship and loss.

I realized that my family was overjoyed by my visit because it meant that those who had left, who had made it to America, still remember them. It allowed them to believe they have a chance of joining that family one day.

I returned to the United States in August and co-founded the Young Afghan-World Alliance (YA-WA), a humanitarian organization focused on understanding and aiding Afghanistan. In Pashto, the word "ya-wa" is the feminine version of the word "one." We are one nation, and we are all part of one world.

A few weeks after my return, the Twin Towers fell. America was jolted out of its forgetfulness, although in a way no one predicted or wanted. Suddenly Afghanistan was very much in the consciousness of the world. War, a frequent visitor to these hospitable people, became an unwanted guest once again. I returned to Afghanistan in December 2001, as the war was coming to a close, to learn that I had lost nineteen members of my extended family in a U.S. raid on a village. The U.S. forces had attacked the village, responding to information that Taliban were there. According to all witnesses, there were no Taliban in that village. When the bombs began to fall, my relatives scattered into the night—men, women, and little children—only to be strafed by bullets fired from low-flying helicopters. Several of them died this way, running for their lives. Ironically, they had come to this village from their home in Kandahar, which they feared would be in the line of fire.

Despite the loss of life, I have supported intervention, even military force if necessary. While it was the actions of non-Afghans in the country that brought the retaliation of the United States, it is at least good that the Taliban have been ousted and that Afghanistan will finally have a chance to decide its own destiny.

I am glad the world is paying attention now and that many people are beginning to help. I am especially touched by the surviving family members of the September 11 attack who have decided to turn their efforts to helping the people of Afghanistan. I have something in common with the relatives of those who died in the World Trade Center—we lost family members in acts of senseless violence. This, along with our shared desire for peace, is our bond. I am fortunate that I have become close to many of these people and have had the privilege of finding more family and love in the face of tragedy. When I look into the eyes of survivors of September 11, I see the same hope I saw in the eyes of people in Afghanistan. It is a hope that persists even through despair.

I intend to participate in rebuilding the country of my people. I am grateful for the help the United States and the world are willing to offer.

One of my greatest hopes is that Mamoon will go to school soon and have all the opportunity in the world, as I have had in America.

NOTES

1. With Dari, one of the two main languages of Afghanistan.

FROM PAWNS TO PRINCIPALS

THE FUTURE OF AFGHAN WOMEN

RINA AMIRI

THE FALL OF THE TALIBAN and the Bonn process have instilled a sense of hope for Afghanistan, and we dare to imagine a future for that country beyond war, violence, and factionalism. The post-Taliban period also has brought international attention to the plight of Afghan women. From Bonn to Brussels to Kabul, Afghans and the international community have expressed unequivocal support for Afghan women.

To facilitate and sustain a program for the restoration of Afghan women's rights, we must move beyond the politics of rhetoric and symbols. Just as gender has become inextricably linked to warfare, so gender must be bound into peace building. This is imperative not just from a moral standpoint but also from strategic and practical ones.

Without the active participation of women, who form more than 50 percent of the population, peace in Afghanistan is doomed to fail. This is the abiding message of the women in this book.

WHO ARE AFGHAN WOMEN?

We begin by asking who Afghan women are and what promises and challenges their situations present. For years Afghan women were seen as a faceless monolith, incapable of advocating for themselves. But since September 11, the world has glimpsed a different picture, a picture of Afghan women acting in the public sector, in professions, in government, in production. Moreover, as Afghan women from the diaspora in the United States, Europe, Pakistan, and Iran have stepped into public view to advocate for their counterparts in Afghanistan, they have also demonstrated a starkly different image as articulate, educated, and empowered women.

The disparate images of Afghan women demonstrate that women's identity is multidimensional, embedded in complex factors. Gender, like all social matters, is intricate, deeply entwined within the fabric of history, culture, and social relations. Thus, the extended family network, ethnicity, religion, language, social class, urban/rural background, education, and political affiliation are factors that need to be taken into account when we analyze the challenges and opportunities that are part of Afghan women's realities.

An illustration of this point is the marked difference between Afghanistan's rural and urban women, who respectively comprise 85 percent and 15 percent of the total female population. Urban women have had more access to formal employment, education, and decision-making positions, although the degree to which women could take advantage of these possibilities was determined largely by the family, which continues to be the single most important institution throughout the country.

In the agricultural sector, women have been involved in the economy on an informal basis, often working side by side with the men in their families. Poverty and geography frequently colluded to limit rural women's access to resources and opportunities. Because of the lack of funds and infrastructure, even during stable periods the central government was unable to provide the vast majority of rural men and women access to basic education and formal roles in the economy.

Politics and war have further complicated the situation of Afghan women, who have long been the pawns in the political agendas of Afghan leaders. Efforts to support and emancipate women have often been led by men as a component of the state's modernization policies. Such gender measures have been challenged repeatedly and often reversed by traditionalists and the conservative orthodoxy, who have seen the public woman as a symbol of modernization and Westernization. Competing factions in the decades of war and unrest have communicated their political stance in the Muslim world through their treatment of women: Traditional forces have secluded women, and modern forces have tried to emancipate them.

Afghan women throughout the country also have been economically dispossessed, excluded from decision-making positions, denied access to education and basic health services, and removed from the public sphere. In addition, continuous conflict has rendered millions of Afghan women refugees. Over 6 million Afghans have resettled in Pakistan, Iran, Europe, the United States, Canada, and Australia. Each of these contexts has created new realities and challenges for Afghan women.

On a positive note, the harsh conditions under which women have had to survive have made them more resourceful, resilient, and innovative than ever before. Thousands of women whose husbands were away at war have had to take leadership roles in their families. In refugee camps in Pakistan and Iran, Afghan women have gained a variety of skills as workers in cottage industries as local entrepreneurs, even as leaders of nongovernmental organizations (NGOs). Many women took advantage of training programs to learn such skills as using a sewing machine to make quilts and garments.

When the Taliban came into power, Afghan women didn't surrender; many went underground. They learned how to organize underground networks for schooling, health services, and trade. Some female doctors, like the legendary General Suhaila Seddiqi, now the interim minister of health, openly defied the Taliban and practiced medicine. Beneath the *burqa,* Afghan women were building a formidable strength. The fall of the Taliban has contradicted the idea that all Afghan women are hopelessly uneducated or resourceless. At this moment significant numbers of women in Afghanistan are coming forward to reclaim their professional roles as doctors, lawyers, teachers, and journalists.

Many Afghan women who emigrated with their families to the United States, Canada, and Europe took advantage of access to higher education to develop vocational skills and enter professions. A number of these women have become key Afghan activists and have been prominent in lobbying for legislation to deny the Taliban international recognition and to support Afghan women.

In international meetings and conferences on the future of Afghanistan, Afghan women from Afghanistan and the diaspora share their vision and promise. If Afghanistan is to be resurrected, these strengths and skills will form a part of the foundation. Afghan women around the world must be integrated into the monumental task of reconstructing and rebuilding every facet of Afghan society.

WHAT ARE OUR ROLES AND RESPONSIBILITIES?

We should be encouraged that there is now a great awareness of the importance of women's roles in peace processes. We may also be reassured by the chorus of voices that have arisen throughout the world demanding the participation of women in the peace and reconstruction of Afghanistan. However, the restoration of Afghan women's rights and their rightful participation in the country's reconstruction will continue to be contested by those who feel threatened by women's roles in the public realm.

Afghanistan has been a conservative country for centuries, with entrenched ideas and values about men's and women's roles. Western approaches to gender issues must be leavened by an understanding of the ways Afghan men and women live and work together and by a sensitivity to the culture and religious contexts of their roles in society. Achieving clarity about Afghan women's issues requires understanding the way Afghan women *themselves* perceive their tribal and community codes and traditions, their religion, and the decision makers in their world.

Another requirement for any sustainable success on the gender issue in Afghanistan is coordination. This means that all individuals and groups working toward gender justice in Afghanistan must share information, develop mutually supportive programs, avoid overlap, network and cooperate among and across sectors, and work together to identify the strengths we each bring to our common struggle. And we must develop knowledge of innovative NGO and United Nations strategies that have been effective in engendering development and reconstruction in Afghanistan.

International organizations and individuals around the world, Afghans in Afghanistan and in the diaspora, we all have a critical role to play. We must work together. Otherwise we risk overloading the Afghan system, pulling the gender issue in different directions, and pitting Afghan women against competing agendas. Our good intentions could undermine Afghan women's efforts and close this narrow window of opportunity.

To avoid this scenario, we must create a space for women within Afghanistan to advocate on their own behalf, and we must place the gender agenda firmly in their hands. International organizations need to provide Afghan women with the tools and the resources to speak on their own behalf. These will also be essential in advocating for political and financial support for women from a wide range of stakeholders and in strengthening, through training, the leadership capacity of women and women's institutions and networks.

In addition, international actors must look inward and demand that their own institutions reflect the gender equity they ask of other countries. For example, the United Nations should require that women participate in all aspects of its mission, including in leadership positions in Afghanistan. Fortunately, Security Council Resolution 1325[1] makes our case. The United Nations must move beyond rhetoric and demonstrate that it will adhere to the international law it has passed by making women an integral part of its political agenda in reconstruction efforts in postwar countries.

Women in the Muslim world also play a critical role in supporting Afghan women. Decades of religious conservatism have left their marks on Afghan society, and during the transition period, it is unlikely that this situation will change very quickly. Often the first step to counter repressive legislation within Muslim societies is for women to develop an understanding of their rights within the context of the Islamic tradition. Islamic scholars and Muslim feminists can serve as leaders in informing the West as well as Afghans of the historical and religious positions that can provide a basis for countering misogynist policies.

Afghan women living in the West can work to bridge the cultural gaps between the Western world and Afghanistan by explaining the needs of Afghan women in the region to non-Afghan leaders and organizations.

Finally, it is critical for Afghan women throughout the diaspora and within Afghanistan to move beyond the politics of ethnicity that has torn the country apart and unify. Competing for scarce resources, opportunities, and positions, we have become accustomed to working alone, sometimes unintentionally undermining each other's efforts. To succeed in our common mission of leveraging Afghan women's positions, we must put an end to competition and divisiveness. We can begin by developing Afghan women's networks within our communities. To create a broad net that will capture Afghan women's skills and resources, we should develop a comprehensive database of professionals throughout the diaspora and within Afghanistan for reconstruction projects.

We have learned in postconflict situations across the world that when women's voices are included, they foster reconciliation, improve relations between former warring parties in local communities, and strengthen and sustain civil society. Women are a moderating force. Thus, the population of Afghan women and girls, who have been the greatest victims of war, represent the greatest promise in the postwar phase. To help Afghan women succeed, we must harness the commitment of every person, institution, and country dedicated to the restoration of the rights of women and to the reconstruction of Afghanistan. Let us unite to release Afghan women from the shackles of history and politics, myths and symbols, and empower them to serve as agents of change.

NOTES

1. Resolution 1325, which the UN Security Council passed on October 24, 2000, calls for increased representation of women in decision-making and peace processes, the protection of women, gender mainstreaming in UN reporting systems, and many other measures that support and protect the human rights of women. The complete document is available at www.un.org/Docs/scres/2000/res1325e.pdf. See "Women Are Opening Doors: Security Council Resolution 1325 in Afghanistan," Felicity Hill and Mikele Aboitiz in this volume.

WOMEN FOR AFGHAN WOMEN— MISSION STATEMENT

Women for Afghan Women (WAW) is an organization of Afghan and non-Afghan women from the New York area who are committed to ensuring the human rights of Afghan women.

WAW promotes the agency of local Afghan women through the creation of safe forums where Afghan women can network, develop programs to meet their specific needs, and participate in human rights advocacy in the international sphere.

WAW raises funds for the reconstruction of Afghanistan, particularly schools and health facilities for women and children. Recognizing that the ability to earn one's living is fundamental to the empowerment of women, WAW supports the development of vocational training programs for women in Afghanistan who have been denied access to education and professional training.

The inclusion of women in all decision-making processes is a requirement of a democratic society. WAW advocates for the representation of women in all areas of life in Afghanistan: political, social, cultural, and economic.

Board of Directors
Marti Copleman
Homaira Mamoor
Sunita Mehta
Zolaykha Sherzad

Afifa Yusufi
Wazhmah Osman

Staff
Masuda Sultan, Program Director

Advisory Committee
Rina Amiri, Senior Associate for Research, Kennedy School of
    Government, Harvard University
Sara Amiryar, Associate Director of Affirmative Action Programs,
    Georgetown University
Helena Malikyar, Research Associate, Center on International
    Cooperation at New York University
Katha Pollitt, journalist, political essayist, and poet
Fahima Vorgetts, Afghan women's rights activist
Sima Wali, President and CEO, Refugee Women in Development

BIBLIOGRAPHY

Books on Afghan Women and Islam

Benard, Cheryl. *Veiled Courage: Inside the Afghan Women's Resistance.* New York: Broadway Books, April 2002.

Doubleday, Veronica. *Three Women of Herat.* New York: F. A. Thorpe Publishing, 1999.

Ellis, Deborah. *Women of the Afghan War.* Westport, CT: Praeger, 2000.

Gauhari, Farooka. *Searching for Saleem.* Foreword by Nancy Dupree. Lincoln: University of Nebraska Press, 1996.

Goodwin, Jan. *Price of Honor: Muslim Women Lift the Veil of Silence on the Islamic World.* New York: Dutton/Plume, 1995.

Khan, Rukhsana. *Roses in My Carpets.* New York: Holiday House, 1998.

Latifa. *My Forbidden Face.* With Shekeba Hachemi and Linda Coverdale. New York: Talk Miramax Books, 2002.

Maggi, Wynne R. *Our Women Are Free: Gender and Ethnicity in the Hindu Kush.* Ann Arbor: University of Michigan Press, 2001.

Mertus, Julie A., and Judy A. Benjamin. *War's Offensive on Women: The Humanitarian Challenge in Bosnia, Kosovo and Afghanistan.* West Hartford, CT: Kumarian Press, 2000.

Skaine, Rosemarie. *Women of Afghanistan Under the Taliban.* Jefferson, NC: McFarland & Co., 2002.

Sulima and Hala. *Behind the Burqa,* as told to Batya Swift Yasgur. New York: John Wiley & Sons (to be published October 2002)

Tapper, Nancy. *Bartered Brides: Politics, Gender and Marriage in an Afghan Tribal Society.* New York: Cambridge University Press, 1991.

Zoya. *Zoya's Story,* with John Follain and Rita Cristofari. New York: William Morrow & Co, 2002

Books about Afghanistan

Adamec, Ludwig W. *Dictionary of Afghan Wars, Revolutions, and Insurgencies.* Foreword by Jon Woronoff. Lanham, MD: Scarecrow Press, 1996.

Ali, Sharifah E. *Afghanistan.* Tarrytown, NY: Marshall Cavendish, Inc., 1995.

Ansary, Mir Tamim. *Afghanistan: Fighting for Freedom.* New York: Dillon Press, 1991.

Bearden, Milton. *Black Tulip: A Novel of War in Afghanistan.* New York: Random House, 2002.

Borovik, Artyom. *The Hidden War: A Russian Journalist's Account of the Soviet War in Afghanistan.* Grove/Atlantic, 2001.

Cooley, John K. K. *Unholy Wars: Afghanistan, America, and International Terrorism.* Sterling, VA: Pluto Press, 2000.

Dupree, Louis. *Afghanistan.* Princeton, NJ: Princeton University Press, 1973.

Edwards, David B. *Heroes of the Age: Moral Fault Lines on the Afghan Frontier.* Berkeley: University of California Press, 1996.

Ellis, Deborah. *The Breadwinner.* Toronto: Douglas & McIntyre, 2001.

Ewans, Martin. *Afghanistan: A Short History of Its People and Politics.* New York: HarperCollins, 2002.

Follett, Ken. *Lie Down with Lions.* New York: Morrow, 1986.

Goodson, Larry P. *Afghanistan's Endless War: State Failure, Regional Politics, and the Rise of the Taliban.* Seattle: University of Washington Press, 2001.

Grazda, Edward. *Afghanistan Diary: 1992–2000.* New York: PowerHouse Books, 2000.

Griffin, Michael. *Reaping the Whirlwind: The Taliban Movement in Afghanistan.* Sterling, VA: Pluto Press, 2000.

Gulzad, Zalmay A. *External Influences and the Development of the Afghan State in the Nineteenth Century.* New York: Peter Lang Publishing, 1995.

Kakar, M. Hassan. *Afghanistan: The Soviet Invasion and the Afghan Response, 1979–1982.* Berkeley: University of California Press, 1997.

Magnus, Ralph H., and Eden Naby. *Afghanistan: Mullah, Marx, and Mujahid.* Boulder, CO: Westview Press, 2000.

Maley, William, ed. *Fundamentalism Reborn?: Afghanistan and the Taliban.* New York University Press, 1998.

Matinuddin, Kamal. *The Taliban Phenomenon: Afghanistan 1994–1997.* Foreword Sahibzada Yaqub Khan. Karachi, Pakistan: Oxford University Press, 1999.

Mayotte, Judy A. *Disposable People?: The Plight of Refugees.* Maryknoll, NY: Orbis Books, 1994.

Nojumi, Neamatollah. *The Rise of the Taliban in Afghanistan: Mass Mobilization, Civil War, and the Future of the Region.* New York: Palgrave, 2002.

Rashid, Ahmed. *Jihad: The Rise of Militant Islam in Central Asia.* New Haven, CT: Yale University Press, 2002.

Roy, Olivier. *Afghanistan: From Holy War to Civil War.* Princeton, NJ: Darwin Press, 1995.

Rubin, Barnett R. *The Search for Peace in Afghanistan: From Buffer State to Failed State.* New Haven, CT: Yale University Press, 2002.

Russian General Staff. *Soviet-Afghan War: How a Superpower Fought and Lost.* Trans. and ed. Lester W. Grau and Michael A. Gress. Lawrence: University Press of Kansas, 2002.

Schultheis, Rob. *Night Letters: Inside Wartime Afghanistan.* Guilford, CT: Lyons Press, 2001.

Shah, Amina. *Tales of Afghanistan.* London: Octagon Press, 1982.

Shah, Sirdar Ikbal Ali, and Ali Ikbal. *Afghanistan and the Afghans.* London: Octagon Press, 1981.

Sheikh, Fazal. *The Victor Weeps: Afghanistan.* New York: Scalo Publishers, 1998.

Tabibi, A. H. *Afghanistan: A Nation in Love.* Chicago: Kazi Publishers, 1978.

ORGANIZATIONS AND RESOURCES

Afghan Women's Organizations

Afghan Women's Educational Center (AWEC)
Palwasha Hassan
Bilal Street, Khalil Road, Academy Town
Peshawar, Pakistan
Tel & Fax: 92–91–841917/43267
E-mail: pal@awn.sdnpk.undp.org

Afghan Women's Mission (AWM)
Steve Penners, Director
260 S. Lake Avenue
P.O. Box 165
Pasadena, CA 91101
Fax: (509)756–2236
Website: info@afghanwomensmission.org

Afghan Women's Network (AWN)
23 Chinar Road, University Town,
Peshawar, Pakistan
Fax: 00 92 91 40436
E-mail: awn@brain.net.pk

Afghan Women's Organization
2333 Dundas Street West, #205
Toronto, Canada
Tel: (416) 588–3585

Afghan Women's Organization of Southern California
Zohra Yusuf Daoud
E-mail: thecaravan@juno.com

Doctors of the World
Flouran Wali
375 West Broadway, 4th floor
New York, NY 10012
Tel: (212) 226–9890
(888) 817-HELP
Website: www.doctorsoftheworld.org

Humanitarian Assistance for the Women and
    Children of Afghanistan (HAWCA)
Orzala Ashraf
P.O. Box 646
G.P.O Peshawar
Pakistan
Tel: 092–91- 811663
Fax: 1–661–4209313
E-mail: hawca@hawca.org

Humanitarian Organization for Orphans and
    Widows of Afghanistan (HOOWA)
Fahima Vorgetts
225 Mill Church Road
Arnold, MD 21012
Tel: (410) 499–3490
E-mail: Fahimav@hotmail.com
Fahimawaw@yahoo.com

Negar
Nasrine Gross
P.O. Box 2079
Falls Church, VA 22042
Tel: (703) 536–6471
E-mail: kabultech@erols.com
negar@wanadoo.fr

Physicians for Human Rights (PHR)
100 Boylston Street, Suite 702
Boston, MA 02116
Tel: (617) 695–0041
Fax: (617) 695–0307
E-mail: www.phrusa.org

Refugee Women in Development (REFWID)
Sima Wali
5225 Wisconsin Avenue NW, Suite 502
Washington, DC 20015
Tel: (703) 931–6442
Fax: (703) 931–5906
E-mail: refwid@erols.com

Revolutionary Association of the Women of Afghanistan (RAWA)
Mehmooda
P.O. Box 374
Quetta, Pakistan
Tel: 0092–300–8551638
E-mail: rawa@rawa.org
Website: www.rawa.org

Women for Afghan Women (WAW)
Masuda Sultan
P.O. Box 152 Midtown Station
New York, NY 10018
Tel: (212) 868–9360
E-mail: info@womenforafghanwomen.org
Website: www.womenforafghanwomen.org

Women for Women of Afghanistan (W4WA)
804 Semlin Drive
Vancouver, BC V5L 4J5
Canada
Tel: (604) 682–3269
E-mail: w4wa.van@lycos.com

Women's Alliance for Peace and Human Rights in Afghanistan (WAPHA)
Zieba Shorish-Shamley
E-mail: info@wapha.org
Website: www.wapha.org

Other Afghan Organizations and Resources

Afghan Communicator
Rameen Moshref
E-mail: YoungAfghans@hotmail.com
Website: www.AfghanCommunicator.com

Afghanistan Online
"All You Ever Wanted to Know about Afghanistan on the Web"
(Comprehensive website on all issues related to Afghanistan plus links to all
    Afghan related sites)
P.O. Box 4867
Foster City, CA 94404
Fax 801–761–5134
E-mail: qazi@afghan-web.com
Website: http://www.afghan-web.com/

School of Hope
Zolaykha Sherzad
269 East 7 Street #3
New York, NY,10009
Tel: (212) 475–8601
E-mail: zolaykha@hotmail.com
Website: www.sohope.org

Society for Aid to Reconstruct Afghanistan (SARA)
Arian Aziz, President
34 Duke Drive
Manhasset Hill, NY 11040
Tel: (516) 627–8995
E-mail: sara@sarainc1.org
Website: www.sarainc1.org

Young Afghan-World Alliance (YA-WA)
Masuda Sultan, President
717 White Plains Road, Suite 224
Scarsdale, NY 10583
Tel: (914) 272–2517
Fax: (914) 931–1788
E-mail: info@YA-WA.org
Website: www.ya-wa.org

Women's Organizations Addressing Afghan Women's Rights

American Jewish World Service
Ruth Messinger, President
45 West 36th Street
New York, NY 10036
Tel: (800) 889–7146

(212) 273–1634
Website: www.ajws.org

Equality Now
Jessica Neuwirth, President
P.O. Box 20646
Columbus Circle Station
New York, NY 10023
E-mail: info@equalitynow.org

Feminist Majority Foundation
Eleanor Smeal, President
1600 Wilson Boulevard, Suite 801
Arlington, VA 22209
Tel: (703) 522–2214
Fax: (703) 522–2219
E-mail: femmaj@feminist.org
Website: www.feminist.org

MADRE
Vivian Stromberg, Executive Director
121 West 27th Street, Room 301
New York, NY 10001
Tel: (212) 627–0444
Fax: (212) 675–3704
E-mail: madre@igc.org
Website: www.madre.org

Sisterhood is Global Institute
4095 Chemin de la Côte-des-Neiges, Suite 12
Montreal, QC, Canada H3H 1W9
Tel: (514) 846–9366
Fax:: (514) 846–9066
E-mail: sigi@qc.aibn.com
Website: www.sigi.org

Tahirih Justice Center
Layli Bashir Miller, Irena Lieberman, Staff Attorneys
P.O. Box 7638
Falls Church, VA 22040
Tel: (703) 237–4554

Fax: (703) 237–4574
Email: justice@tahirih.org
Website: www.tahirih.org

United Nations Development Fund for Women (UNIFEM)
Noeleen Heyzer, Executive Director
304 East 45th Street, 15th floor
New York, NY 10017
Tel: (212) 906–6400
Fax: (212) 906–6705
Website: http://www.unifem.undp.org

V-Day
Eve Ensler, Founder
E-mail: info@vday.org
Website: www.vday.org

Women Living Under Muslim Laws (WLUML)
Website: www.wluml.org

Women Waging Peace/Women and Public Policy Program
Harvard University
John F. Kennedy School of Government
Ambassador Swanee Hunt
79 JFK Street
Cambridge, MA 02138
Tel: (617) 495–8246
Fax: (617) 496–6154
Website: www.womenwagingpeace.net

CONTRIBUTOR BIOGRAPHIES

MURWARID ABDIANI was born in Kabul, Afghanistan, in 1976. She is the niece of Zohra Yusuf Daoud, also a contributor to this volume. Ms. Abdiani has a degree in Film Studies from the University of California, Santa Barbara. She has interned at ABC News and has written for *The Independent*, an arts and entertainment newspaper in Santa Barbara, California.

MIKELE ABOITIZ was born and raised in Uruguay. She has lived in New York City for the last three years, where she has been working for the Women's International League for Peace and Freedom's United Nations Office and its PeaceWomen Project. She is currently working on a master's degree in Business Administration at Fordham University.

RINA AMIRI was born in Afghanistan and was forced to flee with her family after political unrest there. Since then she has resided in Pakistan, India, and the United States. Ms. Amiri is actively working with the Afghan Diaspora community to establish sustainable peace. In November 1999 she served as one of the organizers for the Emergency Committee of the *Loya Jirga* (Peace Assembly) in Rome. She is a member of the Afghan Women's Network and an advisor to the Afghan Women's Educational Center in Pakistan. Ms. Amiri was one of the chief architects of Women Waging Peace, a network of women peace-builders from around the world. Ms. Amiri is currently the Senior Associate for Research at Harvard's Kennedy School of Government. She serves on Women for Afghan Women's Advisory Committee.

SARA AMIRYAR received her bachelor's degree from Kabul University and her master's degree from Georgetown University in International Affairs. She is currently the Associate Director of Affirmative Action Programs, the Coordinator of the Americans with Disabilities Act, and a Certified Mediator at Georgetown University. She is the Vice President of the Central Asia Research and Development Center. Ms. Amiryar served as President of the Afghan Association for Solidarity and Cooperation from 1994 to 1996. She participated in the Afghan Women's Summit for Democracy as well as the UNIFEM Conference on Afghanistan in Brussels, December 2001. Ms. Amiryar serves on Women for Afghan Women's Advisory Committee.

FRESHTA AMIRZADA was born in Kabul in 1979 and grew up in the United States, practicing Islam and writing poetry. She graduated from Queens College with a bachelor's degree in Psychology and Elementary Education. She lives in Queens, New York, with her parents and twin sister.

FEVZIYE RAHZOGAR BARLAS was born in Mazaar-e-Sharif. She grew up in Turkey and attained a bachelor's degree in Turkish and English Languages and Literatures at the University of Istanbul. She has a Master's Degree in Near Eastern/Middle Eastern Languages from the University of Washington, Seattle, where she is a doctoral candidate in the Near East/Middle East Interdisciplinary Program. She writes poetry in Persian, Turkish, and English.

ZOHRA YUSUF DAOUD was the first and last woman to hold the title of Miss Afghanistan (1972–2002). She currently lives in Malibu, California, and hosts a talk show, *24 Hour Voice of Afghanistan*. Ms. Daoud frequently organizes events celebrating Afghan art and culture and is Director of Culture and Communications of the Afghan Women's Association of Southern California.

ATIA GAHEEZ was born in 1971 in Kabul, Afghanistan. She attended the Kabul Medical Institute until 1996, when the Taliban came to power and the college was closed. Ms. Gaheez came to the United States in October 1998. She is currently a student at the University of Baltimore and plans to major in English.

ELIZABETH GOULD AND PAUL FITZGERALD This wife-and-husband team were the first American journalists to acquire permission to enter Afghanistan behind Soviet lines in 1981 for CBS News. In 1982 they produced *Afghanistan Between Three Worlds,* a one-hour documentary for PBS. In 1983 they returned to Kabul for ABC *Nightline.* Their novel *The Voice,* which focuses on he mystical side of their Afghanistan experience, was published in January 2001. Their book *Afghanistan: The End of Illusion* was completed in 2001. Their essay in this volume is an excerpt from the book they are currently writing called *The Apostle's Diary.*

RIFFAT HASSAN is a feminist Muslim theologian, philosopher, and professor of Religious Studies and Humanities at the University of Louisville, Kentucky. Originally from Pakistan, Dr. Hassan is world renowned as a liberal, modernist Muslim thinker, who has done pioneer work in the areas of women in Islam, human rights from a Qur'anic perspective, and inter-religious dialogue. In 1999 Dr. Hassan founded The International Network for the Rights of Female Victims of Violence in Pakistan to launch a worldwide movement for the elimination of "honor" crimes and other forms of violence against girls and women in Pakistan.

FELICITY HILL was, until recently, the Director of the UN office of Women's International League for Peace and Freedom. Ms. Hill's activism began in 1988 with free education campaigns and went on to cover such issues as violence against women, preserving forests, opposing private prisons, the export of arms and uranium from Australia, and exposing police violence.

ESTHER HYNEMAN spent her professional life teaching literature, Women's Studies and Gender Studies at the Brooklyn Campus of Long Island University. She retired from the classroom last August. She now devotes much of her time to her painting, where she struggles to combine her interest in realism, her appreciation for the way women have been rendered in Western art, her commitment to feminism, and her belief in the transformative power of visual beauty. She joined WAW last October when searching for a way to turn her long frustration about the women of Afghanistan into practical action.

ANGELA E. V. KING is Assistant Secretary-General and Special Advisor on Gender Issues and Advancement of Women, by appointment of Secretary-General Mr. Kofi Annan. She chairs the Inter-Agency Committee of Women and Gender Equality and supervises the Division of Advancement of Women. Ms. King joined the UN Secretariat in 1966 from the Permanent Mission of Jamaica, where she was one of the first two women foreign service officers posted after Jamaica joined the United Nations. She participated in the first UN Conference on Women in Mexico City in 1975 and the second UN Conference on Women in Copenhagen in 1980. She represented the Secretariat at the Fourth World Conference on Women at Beijing in 1995.

ANDREA LABIS is a psychotherapist, writer, and women's rights activist. Her personal goals of seeing violence against women and girls a thing of the past and gender equality a thing of the present and future keep her motivated in her years-long devotion to the women of Afghanistan. Andrea trained as a Clinical Social Worker and maintains a private practice in New York City, where she bears witness to others healing from the effects of rape, incest, and sexual abuse. She hopes that someday there will be no need for her services.

ARLINE J. LEDERMAN lived in Kabul and taught at Kabul University for more than six years, starting in 1965. Most recently, in April 2002, she returned for an evaluation trip. A specialist in the traditional arts of Afghanistan, Dr. Lederman traveled throughout the country on a Fulbright Fellowship in 1977–78 as the last Western researcher permitted to travel at that time. In 1978, she co-founded the Afghanistan Relief Committee, which worked to provide humanitarian aid and helped shape U.S. foreign policy to provide assistance to the people of Afghanistan. Dr. Lederman continues to work for the betterment of society in Afghanistan, a place she dearly loves.

IRENA LIEBERMAN is the Director of Legal Services at the Tahirih Justice Center. As the center's first full-time attorney, she directs their three legal programs: the Afghan Refugee Project, the Gender-Based Asylum and Immigration Project, and the Battered Immigrant Women's Advocacy Project. The granddaughter of refugees from the holocaust, Ms. Lieberman has represented immigrants and refugees before the Immigration and Naturalization Service, the Immigration Court, and the Board of Immigration Appeals in matters involving gender-based international human rights abuses including honor crimes, female genital mutilation, rape, trafficking, domestic violence, and forced marriage. Recently, Ms. Lieberman served as co-counsel for oral arguments before the Board of Immigration Appeals in a precedent-setting case. A graduate of American University's Washington College of Law, she has been featured on live radio shows, quoted in the Washington, D.C., *Legal Times* and other media. Most recently she appeared on *CNN World Report.*

HOMAIRA MAMOOR was born in Kabul, Afghanistan. When she was ten years old, her family migrated to the United States. She received her bachelor's degree, married an enlightened Afghan man, and has three daughters. After September 11, she became an activist on behalf of Afghan women. Ms. Mamoor is a board member of Women for Afghan Women. She is an active member of the Islamic Center of New York and is currently involved with a new initiative in New York called the Muslim Reformist Movement, which studies Islamic ideals and principles in a contemporary context and seeks to free Islam from cultural influences. Ms. Mamoor is also pursuing a master's degree in Women's Studies and Theology.

WEEDA MANSOOR is a member of the Revolutionary Association of the Women of Afghanistan (RAWA). She is thirty-five years old, married, and has three children. She joined RAWA in its early years when its martyred leader Meena was alive. Ms. Mansoor has extensive experience of underground work in Afghanistan.

SUNITA MEHTA is Director of Grants and Programs at The Sister Fund, a feminist foundation in New York City. She serves on the Boards of SAKHI for South Asian Women and Center for Anti-Violence Education, both New York–based women's antiviolence organizations. Ms. Mehta co-founded Women for Afghan Women in April 2001. She was born in India, and raised in India and England. She lives in Brooklyn, New York, with her husband and two young sons.

RUTH MESSINGER is President of the American World Jewish Service and former Borough President of Manhattan. She has been included in *The Forward*'s listing of the top fifty Jewish personalities in America. In 1997 she was the first woman to secure the Democratic Party nomination for mayor of New York.

SANAA NADIM is the Muslim chaplain of the interfaith center at the State University of New York, Stonybrook. Originally from Egypt, she is currently a member of the Multi-Faith Forum of Long Island, the Advisory Board of WLIW Channel 21, and the Islamic Association of Long Island. Sister Nadim is a speaker and lecturer on Islamic issues and women's rights in Islam.

FARIBA NAWA was born in Herat, Afghanistan, and moved to the United States at the age of ten. She is a graduate student at New York University. A freelance journalist, she writes for *Mother Jones,* the *Village Voice,* the *San Francisco Chronicle,* the Pacific News Service, and Agence France Presse. She is also a correspondent for Free Speech Radio News on Pacifica Radio.

LINA PALLOTTA is an Italian photographer based in New York City. She studied Documentary and Photojournalism at the International Center of Photography in New York. Since 1991 she has been working as a contributing photographer for the photo agency Grazia Neri and the Impact Visuals agency in New York. She photographs extensively in the Lower East Side, where she lives. She was awarded "The Catalogue Project 1998" grant by the New York Foundation for the Arts for her ongoing project, "Piedras Negras," about Mexican women working in the *maquilladoras.*

ZOHRA RASEKH is Senior Research Associate for Global Watch Group. In Spring 2001 Ms. Rasekh headed a medical fact-finding team to assess the health and human rights of Afghan women and children in northern Afghanistan, areas under the control of the Taliban opposition. She is coauthor of the book *The Taliban's War on Women: A Health and Human Rights Crisis in Afghanistan,* published in 1998 by Physicians for Human Rights.

ELEANOR SMEAL is President of the Feminist Majority Foundation. For over thirty years, she has been on the frontlines fighting for women's equality in the United States. Ms. Smeal served as President of the National Organization for Women from 1977 to 1982 and 1985 to 1987. In this capacity, she led the drive to ratify the Equal Rights Amendment and also led the first national abortion rights march in 1986, drawing more than 100,000 participants to Washington, D.C. Expanding her feminist activities to a global level, in 1997 she launched the Campaign to Stop Gender Apartheid in Afghanistan.

GLORIA STEINEM is listed in *Biography Magazine* as one of the twenty-five most influential women in America. She is a frequent spokeswoman on issues of equality. As founder of *Ms. Magazine,* she is one of the most influential writers, editors, and activists of our time. She is the author of *Outrageous Acts and Everyday Rebellions,* a collection of essays (1983); *Revolution from Within: A Book of Self-Esteem* (1993); and *Moving Beyond Words/Age, Rage, Sex, Power, Money, Muscles: Breaking the Boundaries of Gender* (1995).

MASUDA SULTAN was born in Kandahar, Afghanistan, in 1978; her family fled to the United States when she was five. Raised in New York City, after receiving her bachelor's degree in Economics she returned to Kandahar in July 2001 to explore her family roots. Founding the Young

Afghan-World Alliance (YA-WA) upon her return, Ms. Sultan has worked on numerous outreach efforts, including leading YA-WA's humanitarian aid efforts in Afghanistan. While filming a documentary in Afghanistan in December 2001, Ms. Sultan learned of the deaths of nineteen members of her extended family in the U.S. bombing campaign. She is currently working with Global Exchange and the families of the victims of the September 11 attacks and is Program Director of Women for Afghan Women.

FAHIMA VORGETTS has been working for many years for women's rights in Afghanistan. In Kabul, she served as director of a women's literacy program and studied chemistry in graduate school. She has testified about Taliban abuses before the United Nations and other organizations. Ms. Vorgetts runs an import business and owns a café on the West Coast, with portions of profits from her businesses going to the women of Afghanistan. She serves on Women for Afghan Women's Advisory Committee.

SIMA WALI is President and Chief Executive Officer of Refugee Women in Development (RefWID), an international institution focusing on women in conflict and postconflict reintegration issues. She is a native of Afghanistan. Her personal experience as a woman and a refugee inspires her work for uprooted women's human rights. She advocates nationally and internationally for refugee women and girls whose rights have been violated. Ms. Wali is the recipient of Amnesty International's 1999 Third Annual Ginetta Sagan Fund Award in recognition of her work on Afghan women and human rights. Ms. Wali serves on Women for Afghan Women's Advisory Committee.

BATYA SWIFT YASGUR, MA, MSW, is a full-time freelance writer of fiction as well as medical non-fiction. She has written or co-authored several books, including *Women at Risk,* which is about cervical disease and the HPV virus, and *America: A Freedom Country* (Lutheran Immigration and Refugee Service), about asylum and detention issues. She is the winner of the Mystery Writers of America's Robert L. Fish Award for Best First Published Mystery Story. Her book, *Behind the Burqa,* by "Sulima" and "Hala" as told to Batya Swift Yasgur, a memoir of two Afghan sisters, is scheduled for publication by John Wiley and Sons, Inc. in fall 2002.

INDEX